Emerging FinTech

Emerging FinTech

Understanding and Maximizing Their Benefits

Paul Taylor, MBA, MBCS, FRSA CMgr FCMI

BUSINESS EXPERT PRESS

Leader in applied, concise business books

Emerging FinTech: Understanding and Maximizing Their Benefits

Cover design by Charlene Kronstedt

Interior design by Exeter Premedia Services Private Ltd., Chennai, India

First published in 2022 by
Business Expert Press, LLC
222 East 46th Street, New York, NY 10017
www.businessexpertpress.com

ISBN-13: 978-1-63742-247-2 (paperback)
ISBN-13: 978-1-63742-248-9 (e-book)

Business Expert Press Service Systems and Innovations for Business and Society Collection

First edition: 2022

10 9 8 7 6 5 4 3 2 1

Description

Financial Services and Technology (FinTech) have collaborated for decades with mutual benefit, and it is not unreasonable to expect this co-operation to continue, especially with the development of emerging technologies.

However, both industries are facing challenges. Financial Services suffer from regulation, client, and risk pressures. Emerging technologies suffer from their inherent complexity and implementation challenges.

It is imperative that Financial Services' firms understand emerging technologies to ensure they are implemented effectively to support both current business and future challenges.

This book takes a pragmatic and critical review of Emerging Technologies exploring

- What the technologies are?
- How they can be used?
- How they can be implemented pragmatically?
- How they could help address future challenges?

This book provides an overview of emerging technologies within Financial Services to allow firms to understand their real benefits and how to pragmatically implement them for maximum benefit.

Keywords

financial services; banking; investment management; asset management; insurance; technology; emerging technology; regulation; clients; products; lack of trust, data; operating models; profit; cost; workforce; competition; risk management; remote working; self-servicing; machine learning; robotic process automation; Internet-of-Things, IoT; natural language processing, NLP; digital currency; cloud computing; big data; green computing; climate change; ESG; trading; payments; FinTech; technology; future challenges

Contents

CHAPTER 1

Introduction

This book discusses and explores 10 emerging technology trends and their impact on the Financial Services industry.

The structure of the book can be split into four main parts:

Part One—Background and Context Setting

The first part starts (in Chapter 2) with a short overview of the Financial Services industry covering the main players which are summarized in Figure 1.1 below. This chapter is not meant to provide an in-depth overview but to provide sufficient context for the rest of the book.

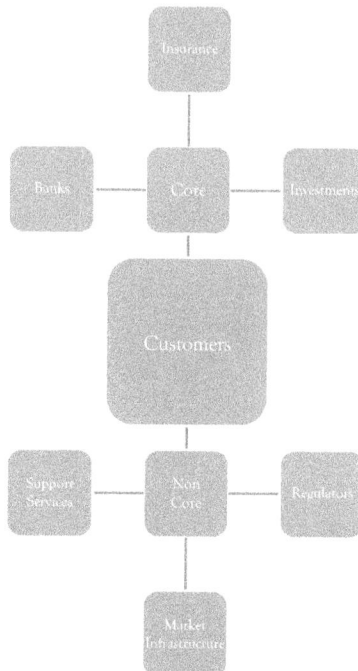

Figure 1.1 High-level summary of the industry

This is followed by (in Chapter 3) a history of the Financial Services industry and how technology has helped or hindered the growth of the industry. Again this chapter is not meant to provide a detailed chronological history with in-depth discussion, but it is to provide a sufficient context to explain how the industry has evolved with a particular nod to technology. This history is summarized in Figure 1.2 below.

Figure 1.2 The four stages of the financial services technology evolution

This first part then concludes (in Chapter 4) with a summary of the key challenges that the Financial Services industry is currently facing. These are summarized in Figure 1.3 below.

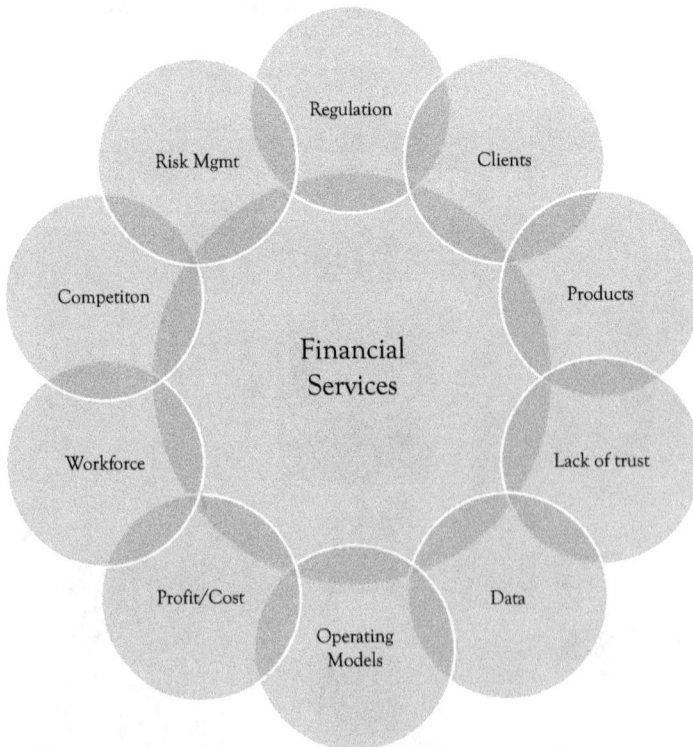

Figure 1.3 Summary of the challenges of impacting the financial services industry

Part Two—Exploring the Impact of the 10 Emerging Technology Trends

The second part is the main part of this book. It contains 10 chapters (from Chapters 5 to 14) with each chapter discussing an individual technology trend and its impact on the Financial Services industry. The 10 trends are summarized in Figure 1.4 below.

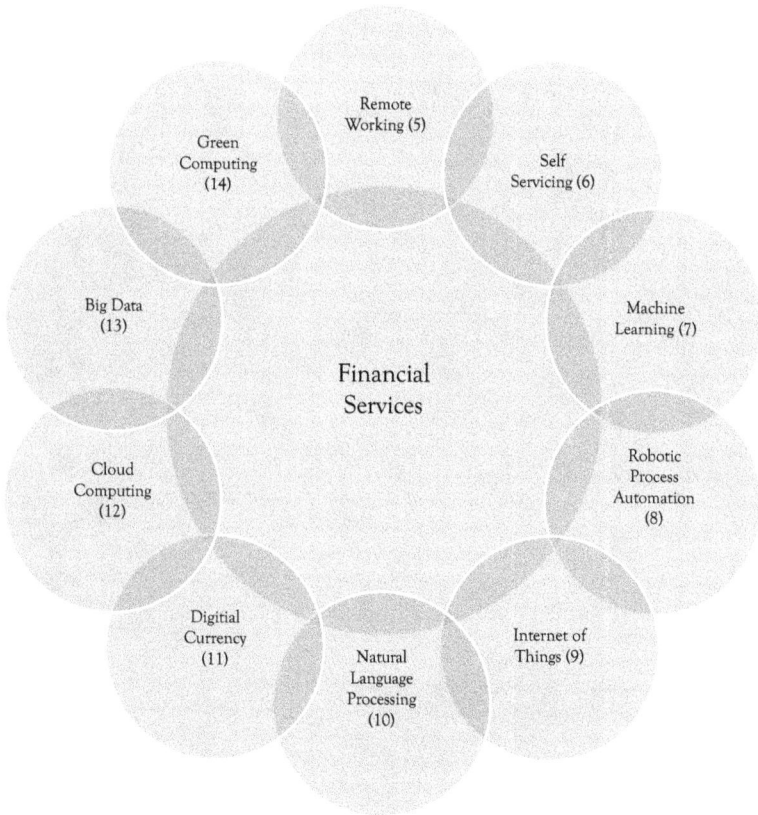

Remote Working (5)

Green Computing (14)

Self Servicing (6)

Big Data (13)

Machine Learning (7)

Financial Services

Cloud Computing (12)

Robotic Process Automation (8)

Digitial Currency (11)

Internet of Things (9)

Natural Language Processing (10)

Figure 1.4 Summary of the 10 technology trends

The structure of each chapter is similar. Initially, an overview of the technology is given with the benefits it can provide at a general level. Then each chapter will discuss how the technology is currently being used within the Financial Services industry followed by a discussion on the pragmatic challenges of implementing and using the technology. This leads to how the technology either helps with or hinders the key industry challenges listed in Chapter 4. Each chapter then ends with a case study followed by a small summary of the key points to aid understanding.

Part Three—Wrap Up and Looking to the Future

The third and final part is a summary of the book outlining the key themes and challenges going forward.

CHAPTER 2

Overview of the Financial Services Industry

This chapter provides a summary of the Financial Services industry. It is not meant to provide an in-depth overview but to provide sufficient context for the rest of the book.

A Simple Definition

The Financial Services industry is a wide and complex area (which this chapter will hopefully demonstrate) which means providing a precise definition can be challenging. Therefore for this book, it will be defined as follows:

> The Financial Industry consists of many Financial Services Organizations providing financial services products/services to their customers and consumers.
>
> The Financial Services Organizations that provide these services cover many firms such as banks, credit card providers, investment managers plus others.
>
> The products/services provided cover offerings such as bank accounts, investment products, credit cards, investment advice, capital funding plus others.
>
> These customers and consumers who receive these products/services will cover everything from individual retail customers to large multinational organizations, local/national governments and pension funds.

Why Is Financial Services Critical?

It is safe to say that the Financial Services industry is critical to the day-to-day operations of the global economy.

The movement of money must happen and if it does not happen then there will be material issues. For example, imagine the situation if invoices, salaries, or pensions were not being paid? There would be uproar, possible rioting, and a general breakdown of society.

Likewise, many activities legally need insurance in place to allow them to happen. For example, a pilot and airline need insurance to fly a plane, people need insurance to drive a car, and people often need to take out insurance before going on holiday.

How Big Is the Financial Services Industry?

Unfortunately, obtaining accurate statistics on the size of the Financial Services industry (or any industry for that matter) is challenging. This is because most assessments are performed using different measurements, using different methodologies, using differing timescales, using different assumptions, and are often performed for different purposes.

However, some high-level statistics can be quoted to demonstrate the size of the global Financial Services industry.

- Forbes in 2019 created a "list of world's largest public firms in revenue generation" which showed Banking as the third biggest industry by sales globally (at USD 4.424 trillion) and Insurance as the sixth biggest industry by sales globally (at USD 2.611 trillion). The top industry was Oil and Gas (at USD 4.797 trillion) with Technology (also a topic of this book) coming in second at USD 4.726 trillion. Therefore, if Banking and Insurance were combined under the umbrella of Financial Services then it would be the largest industry by sales globally.
- The same study also assessed profitability by industry and Banking was top of the list at USD 773 million with Technology second (at USD 548 billion) and Oil and Gas third (at USD 292 billion). Insurance, in this case, was much further down the list with a profitability of USD 148 billion.

This means it is safe to say that Financial Services (and Technology for that matter) is one of the world's largest industries in terms of revenue and profitability.

The Structure of the Financial Services Industry

Figure 2.1 provides a high-level summary of the main areas of the industry.

At the center of the industry is (or should always be) the customer because ultimately they are the people which the industry is trying to service. Without customers, the industry would not exist. This area is discussed in more detail further below.

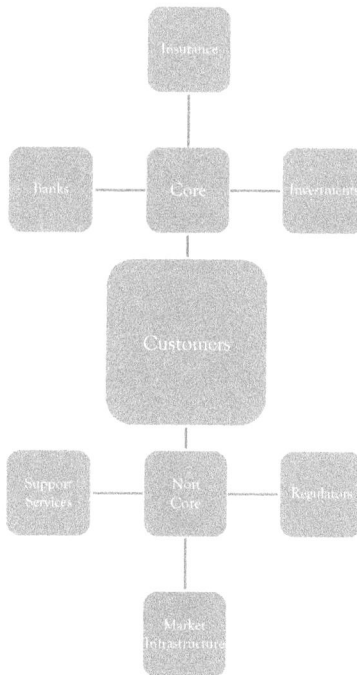

Figure 2.1 High-level summary of the industry

Around the customers, there are a variety of industry players which can be split into "core" players and "non-core" players namely:

- "Core" players are the organizations that provide actual
  financial products and services to customers. These
  organizations are Banks, Insurance (and Pension) Companies,
  and Investors. These are discussed in more detail below.

- "Non-core" players are other key industry members but these provide support services to the industry and do not provide actual services or products to the customers or consumers. These cover organizations such as Technology firms, Legal firms, Infrastructure, and Regulators. These are discussed in more depth below.

Customers

A customer can be any person or organization that can exist globally. For example, these could be individual people, partnerships, charities, organizations, and government bodies. Customers are the group who the industry is supposed to serve but (as this book will demonstrate) this is much more challenging than it sounds. This is because firms are often diverted away from serving their customers due to regulatory challenges, operating model complexities, the challenges of "going green," the need to make a return for their shareholders plus many others.

Core Players

At the simplest level, there are three types of core players within the Financial Services industry.

Banks

This group is probably the most common and prominent with (a) most people in the developed world having at least one bank account product and (b) most villages, towns, or cities having several different bank branches located within them.

Banking itself can be split into further subgroups, namely:

- Retail, Consumer, or Personal Banking
- Business Banking
- Investment Banking

Each is discussed below.

Retail, Consumer, or Personal Banking

These banks provide services and products to the general public or retail customers which are distributed via branches, websites, and call centers. They offer a range of generic services such as

- Current accounts—An account at a bank where money can be deposited and withdrawn without notice.
- Savings accounts—An account at a bank where a small amount of interest is paid on the amount deposited. Typically, there is no notice for adding or removing monies.
- Mortgages—A legal agreement where a bank will loan money (with interest) to allow an individual to purchase a property. The mortgage loan is guaranteed by the property so if the borrower defaults then the bank can take legal title of the property. However, once the mortgage is fully paid then the bank has no claim over the property.
- Personal loans—A loan from a bank to an individual for a personal need (such as buying a car).
- Debit cards—A debit card is a payment card that deducts money from the customer's current account when it is used. It can be used to purchase goods or withdraw cash from an ATM.
- Credit cards—A card that allows a customer (or the cardholder) to borrow money to pay for goods and services. The customer will be charged interest on the borrowed money and sometimes they will also be charged a flat fee as well. The customer will be expected to refund the borrowed money back to the bank regularly.

Also, some countries allow Savings Institutions to exist (such as Building Societies within the UK or Credit Unions in other parts of the world). These will offer similar (if not the same services and products) as Retail Banks. However, the main difference is that Retail Banks are normally owned by shareholders whereas Savings Institutions are owned by their customers. For this reason, they are sometimes called Mutual.

Business Banking

This is similar to Retail Banking but these organizations offer services to corporations and other larger clients. These services are also distributed via Branches, Websites, and Call Centers. Some Banks will offer both Retail and Business Banking through the same Branch (although Business Banking does tend to be performed from larger branches situated in towns and cities). They offer similar services as Retail Banking (see above) but they are tailored more towards corporations. The list of typical services is listed below again for completeness

- Current accounts—An account at a bank where money can be deposited and withdrawn without notice.
- Savings accounts—An account at a bank where a small amount of interest is paid on the amount deposited. Typically, there is no notice for adding or removing monies.
- Mortgages—A legal agreement where a bank will loan money (with interest) to allow an individual to purchase a property. The mortgage loan is guaranteed by the property so if the borrower defaults then the bank can take legal title of the property. However, once the mortgage is fully paid then the bank has no claim over the property.
- Personal loans—A loan from a bank to an individual for a personal need (such as buying a car).
- Debit cards—A debit card is a payment card that deducts money from the customer's current account when it is used. It can be used to purchase goods or withdraw cash from an ATM.
- Credit cards—A card that allows a customer (or the card-holder) to borrow money to pay for goods and services. The customer will be charged interest on the borrowed money and sometimes they will also be charged a flat fee as well. The customer will be expected to refund the borrowed money back to the bank regularly.

Investment Banking

This area is often misunderstood but effectively it is a bank that performs complex, risky, and large transactions on behalf of large customers such as companies, institutions, and governments. It will offer most of the basic banking services (detailed under Retail and Business Banking above) as well as the following specialist services:

- Raising of Capital—This is trying to raise capital (or money) for its corporate customers. This could involve acting as the "middle man" to match companies who want to issue shares with investors who want to buy them.
- Mergers and Acquisitions—This involves helping customers who want to merge and acquire companies. Specifically, this could cover providing advice, performing research, executing due diligence, negotiating to fund, negotiating contracts, and finding investors.
- Securities sales and trading (across bonds, equities, derivatives, foreign exchange, and other asset classes)—This involves providing books of shares that can be traded with other firms such as other Investment Banks or Asset Managers. These securities are normally trading on behalf of the bank themselves and this is often called propriety trading. This is different to Investment Managers, who trade on behalf of their clients and customers (and this is often called Agent or Agency trading).
- Providing Banking Services for large organizations such as governments and multinational firms. These types of firms will have complex and demanding banking needs (such as large short-term borrowing needs, large transaction amounts, or complex liabilities that need to be managed) which will need support and are far too complex and risky for standard Retail or Business Banks.

Insurance

The concept behind insurance is relatively straightforward. At its simplest level, insurance is a product or service to mitigate against the risk of something nasty happening (often with an associated financial or another type of loss). The party which could be impacted will pay a cash premium to an insurance firm who will then pay a financial amount to re-compensate this party if the event happens. The size of the premium is dependent on the size of the compensation and the likelihood of the event happening. For example, for a large compensation which is likely to happen then the premium will be large whereas for small compensations with a low likelihood then the premium will be smaller.

The types of events that could happen are vast, namely:

- Death—On the death of the insured person then a pre-agreed amount of money will be paid to the policyholders (who are typically family members of the person who has died). In the UK, this is often termed Life Assurance (as opposed to Insurance) to reflect the fact that death will happen as opposed to Insurance which is to mitigate against an event that could happen.
- Critical illness insurance—In this insurance plan, the insurer will pay a lump sum and/or a series of regular payments if the policyholder is diagnosed with one of the specific illnesses detailed in the pre-agreed insurance policy.
- Accident insurance—The policyholder is paid either a lump sum or a set of regular payments if they are injured per the terms of the pre-agreed insurance policy.
- Car (or Vehicle) Insurance—This provides financial insurance against vehicle damage, bodily injuries, and the personal liability that could result from a traffic accident. Some policies may also cover damage to the vehicle caused by events other than traffic accidents such as theft, vandalism, natural disasters, and others. In many countries, it is illegal to drive a vehicle without suitable insurance in place.
- Home or Buildings Insurance—This insurance provides financial support to losses that could happen to a customer's home such as replacing damaged contents, refunding any extra living expenses, and so on.
- Plus many others such as Agricultural, Flood, Pet, Travel, Income Projection, Cyber, Rent Guarantee, Profession Indemnity, and Personal Indemnity insurance.

However, it cannot stressed be enough how important the Insurance industry is to the day-to-day running of the global economy. This is because many activities cannot take place unless Insurance is in place. For example, individuals need insurance to drive a car, airlines and pilots need insurance to fly their planes, and individuals need professional and personal insurance to perform their work.

Finally, there is a subset of the insurance industry called Reinsurance which is when an insurance firm realizes they have too much exposure to a type of risk then they will look to re-insurance this risk with another insurance firm.

Investments

Investments is an industry where one party (often called the manager) manages investments (such as securities, cash, property, etc.) on behalf of another party (often called the "investor") against a set of agreed objectives (such as increased value by × percent or track a certain benchmark) as well as an agreed set of constraints (such as do not invest in tobacco or carbon polluting stocks). However, it is important to note that this is an agency arrangement and the managers themselves will not invest their own money.

There are two main types of product groups within the industry, namely:

- Collective investment schemes—The manager will pool all investments into a single portfolio which is unitized and then the units are sold to investors. Collective investment schemes are often referred to as Mutual Funds or just Funds in some cases.
- Standalone or segregated portfolio where an individual portfolio is created for each investor and the Manager will purchase and sell investments, specifically for this client who holds this segregated portfolio. These segregated portfolios can be sub-divided further into execution-only (where the investor will decide what to purchase and the manager will follow that order), advisory (where the investor and manager will work together to determine what investments should be bought and/or sold), and discretionary (where the investors

effectively hands over control to the manager who, subject to pre-agreed objectives, will buy, and/or sell investments).

There are four main roles within Investments, namely:

- Investors—The organizations or entities that legally own the assets which are managed. This will cover a wide range of entities from large Sovereign Wealth Funds or Pension Funds down to Retail clients. Retail investors come in many shapes and sizes ranging from an individual who invests a small amount per month into some type of savings plan or collective investment scheme, to day traders and to Retail Clients who are wealthy enough to warrant their segregated portfolio.
- Managers are the entities that manage the assets owned by the Investors via a Collective Investment Scheme or Standalone Segregated Portfolio.
- Distributors are the bodies that are responsible for "distributing" the products that the Manager offers to the Investors. These distributors can cover anything from an individual providing advice on a 1-2-1 basis to complex online platforms which support many products and provide a range of advice and trading services.
- Administrators are responsible for performing all the "day-to-day" administration and operational tasks involved in managing the funds and the underlying investments.

Overlap Between Banks, Insurance, and Investment Firm

While the above three sections list these players separately, there is a large amount of overlap and interaction between them. For example, it is not uncommon for a single firm to own a Retail Bank, Business Bank, Investment Bank, Insurance firm, and Investment firm. These often trade under the same name which creates confusion.

Likewise, it is also not that uncommon that the Retail Bank part of a firm will distribute (or sell) investment products (such as Collective Investment Schemes) that its Investment Firm subsidiary manages.

Furthermore, an Insurance Firm or large Asset Owner (such as a pension fund) may have their captive Investment Firm to manage their assets.

This interaction and overlap caused contamination issues during the credit crisis when issues with Investment Banks spread into Insurance Firms and Retail Banks and almost brought the entire financial system to its knees. (This is discussed in more detail below.)

"Non-Core" Players

There is a wide range of "non-core" players who provide a support service to the industry.

Regulators

Before the Credit Crisis in 2008, financial regulation tended to be very "light touch" compared to other crucial industries. However, since 2008, there has been a "tsunami" of new regulations which has inundated the Financial Services industry. This regulation sets out to ensure that the stability and integrity of the financial system are maintained as well as ensuring consumers are protected and market confidence is maintained. This wave of new and updated regulation is set to continue for the foreseeable future. This complex set of existing and new global regulations is and will continue to provide many challenges to the industry. For example, increased costs to comply which is squeezing profit margins, an adverse impact on innovation, and increased complexity. These challenges are in turn forcing the industry to change the way they work. Firms now need to constantly review cultures, capital requirements, product development processes, investment strategies, marketing approaches, distribution, their operating model, and associated infrastructures as well developing the ability to complete regulatory returns.

Examples of regulators are the Financial Conduct Authority (FCA) in the UK and the Central Bank of Ireland (CBI) in the Republic of Ireland.

Market Infrastructure

This is an area that is often overlooked.

The key point to note is that the financial services industry is almost entirely reliant on technology (which is a key theme of this book). This covers firms operating within their boundaries (such as maintaining accounting records, performing transactions, and servicing customers) as well as firms interacting with each other regularly (such as trading between firms or transferring money between organizations).

To allow this cross-firm interaction to take place between firms then a shared market infrastructure is required (supported by common standards) which firms can "plug into" as required. For example, SWIFT for messaging, BACS for UK payments, exchanges for trading, and many others.

Support Services

Finally, as part of the industry, there are various support or ancillary players who work in the industry but are not financial services in the strictest sense. This cover the following:

- Technology firms—As mentioned previously, all firms are very reliant on technology and the majority of this is provided by external vendors. This technology can range from applications (such as order management systems), networking infrastructure (such as Internet connectivity), data storage providers (such as data centers or cloud providers) plus many others.
- Legal firms and other legal advisors—Firms are reliant on legal firms to support a wide range of legal areas. Financial services are now governed by a complex set of regulations which means firms are reliant on legal firms to ensure they understand the rules so they can be compliant. Furthermore, firms need external legal firms to help support many other areas such as client contracts, supplier contracts, trading agreements, and so on.
- Consultants—Firms will use consultants for a wide range of purposes. This advice could cover areas such as implementing new technology, advice on launching new products, advice on entering new geographic regions, understanding the impact of political decisions, staff contracts, and so on.

- Academia—Firms will often use academia in various areas. This can cover purchasing and using secondary research to help understand how the industry is developing, how client behaviors are changing, understanding how new technology is impacting the industry plus many other areas. Firms will also employ academics to gather primary research on specific issues that are pertinent to the firm; for example, how will economic conditions impact their client base or product range.
- Training firms—The Financial Services industry is a complex industry covering many specific technical skillsets (banking, investments, technology, etc.) and many general skillsets (leadership, staff management, etc.). Staff need to be trained with these skills and firms will often employ specialist training firms for this.
- Recruitment firms—The Financial Services industry employs a large number of people covering permanent staff, contracting staff, part-time staff, and so on. To ensure their staffing needs are met, the firms will employ specialist recruitment firms.
- Trade Associations—These bodies tend to have two main purposes. The first purpose is to holistically represent the industry to outsiders. For example, during the UK's exit from the European Union ("Brexit") between 2016 and 2020, many of the UK Financial Services Trade Association would represent their members and their views to EU and UK governments. It was thought that having a single body (i.e., the Trade Association) with the weight of its member behind it, would carry more gravitas than each firm acting on its own. The second purpose is to allow firms to work together for the general good of the industry. For example, if there is new regulation being implemented then it is not uncommon for Trade Associations to form working groups to allow a large number of firms to work collectively to implement the regulation successfully across the industry.
- There is also a vast number of other support services such as marketing agencies, advertisement agencies, press relations firms, facilities management firms, and others.

CHAPTER 3

A Short History of the Financial Services and How Technology Has Helped and Hindered

This chapter builds on top of the first chapter by providing a chronological history of how the industry has evolved over the past 50 years albeit with a heavy focus on how technology has helped (and, in some cases, hindered) this development. (This chapter is not meant to provide a detailed chronological history with in-depth discussion, but to provide a sufficient context for this book by explaining how the industry has evolved with a particular nod to technology.)

This development can be summarized in the following four stages which do have a certain amount of overlap.

Stage 1 – Pre historic – Up and until the end of the 1970s

Stage 2 – Let's automate these clunky process – 1971 to 1995

Stage 3 – Customers are now going online – 1995 to 2005

Stage 4 – Customer are now leading the industry and going mobile – 2005 onwards.

Figure 3.1 The four stages of the financial services technology evolution

Each of these stages is discussed in more detail below but it is interesting to note that the development of the financial services industry and technology is very much a two-way development process. As technology has grown then it has allowed the financial services industry to expand. For example, using web/mobile to support self-service gives customers more functionality, and allows firms to have more clients as opposed to requiring large call centers and supporting manual processes. Also, financial services have always been a keen user of technology and this use has helped drive the development of the technology holistically. For example, some of the earliest users of relational databases and certain aspects of Artificial Intelligence were Financial Services firms.

Stage 1—Prehistoric up and Until the End of the 1970s

Originally, financial services was a very manual process with records maintained manually with manual book keeping which was laborious, slow, clumsy, and prone to human error. Consequently, people did not use many financial services products. While some people may have had a bank account but little in terms of savings or insurance products. Transactions tended to be performed using cash. Likewise, because of the cumbersome manual nature of the industry, the firms could only offer simple products with minimal functionality.

While there was some technology in place, it was very primitive and not widely used:

1. In 1844, the Telegraph was rolled out across the United States. This allowed simple messages to be sent from one side of the United States to another. However, its use was limited, it needed specific hardware, it needed humans at both ends, and it was prone to error.
2. In 1865, the Pantelegraph was rolled in France. This was effectively the first facsimile machine. Again its use was limited, it needed specific hardware, it needed humans at both ends, and it was prone to error.
3. In 1866, the first trans-Atlantic cable was laid between the UK and the United States. This was a major step forward because it allow messages to be sent within hours as opposed to physically sending the message via ship.
4. Finally, in 1918, the Fedwire Funds Service was implemented by the Federal Reserve Banks. This allowed banks to transfer money between all 12 connected Banks. It used a Morse code system.

However, during the 1950s and 1960s, there was a growth in technology.

Previously with analogue technology, all computers were physically enormous, slow to operate, and unreliable. However, the discovery of digital technology allowed several step progressions with technology to be made. Firstly, it allowed more powerful hardware (such as mainframe computers and mini-computers) to be developed, which apart from being physically smaller and more reliable provided a massive increase in processing power. This, in turn, allowed more advanced and easier to use software languages to be developed as opposed to complex and hard to program languages such as assembler or machine. Many of these languages were designed with a specific business purpose in mind. For example, COBOL for business and FORTRAN for scientific calculations. Secondly, inter-computer communication was improved by the roll-out of some (albeit limited) communication standards.

These developments triggered many changes for Financial Services firms.

1. Firstly, several internal improvements were made. Book-keeping records were automated, thus removing the manual overheads and operational risks of maintaining manual paper ledgers.
2. Secondly, it allowed several new products to be offered to customers.

In the 1950s, the Bank of America launched its first Credit Card (called the BankAmericard) in California, United States. This would become the first recognized Credit Card.

In 1960, the Electronic Pricing Data firm (based in Los Angeles) launched its Quotron Systems. This was the first electronic system to provide stock market quotations to an individual through desktop (albeit bulky) terminals. It also printed up-to-the-minute prices out on ticker tape.

In the 1960s, the first set of Automated Teller Machines (ATMs) was implemented. These allowed customers to obtain balances and withdraw money from a "hole in the wall" without the need to visit a branch. The first withdrawal was made in Enfield, London in the UK in 1967. One could argue that this is the first customer service offering within the financial services industry.

While these developments sound very primitive compared to the technology available now, they were at the time massive breakthroughs. However, these services were costly which did not make them available to the general public. Also (and this is a common theme for all new technology) there was a certain social reluctance to use the technology because the general public did not trust them. It took several years for the general public to be happy to use them.

Stage 2—Let's Automate Those Clunky Processes—1971 to 1995

This period covered a massive step increase in the power of technology although most of the benefits were to the inner workings of the firm with limited benefits to the customers.

This growth has often been linked to Moore's Law. This law (stated by Gordon Moore who was one of the founders of the chip maker Intel) said that the number of transistors increased on an integrated circuit could be doubled approximately every two years. This means that processing power can be doubled every two years as well. This rule allowed a large number of step developments to take place, namely:

1. The processing power of mainframes and minis increased dramatically which allowed more complex operations and functions to be supported. The use of minis become more popular because they were easier to operate than mainframes and they were cheaper to operate.
2. The invention of the personal computer (PC) was in the early 1980s. IBM created the first PC but it was superseded by a flood of cheaper and often more powerful clones. All of these were running MS-DOS which meant applications written for one manufacturer of PC could run across all PC clones. This then allowed an explosion of powerful and easy-to-use packages. This covered spreadsheets, data analysis, and word processors. The growth of PCs started to reduce the demand for mainframes and mini-computers.

3. There were further advances in programming languages on mainframes, minis, and PCs. These languages were easier to use and provided much better functionality.

4. Database technologies also improved and become easier to implement and use. Previously, databases were a collection of clumsy sequential indexed files which were hard to use, maintain, and integrate with. However, Relational Database Management Systems had now become mainstream because they were easy to use, easy to understand, and easy to maintain.

5. The concept of the graphical user interface (GUI) was developed which allowed the user to intuitively interact with a computer using a mouse and set of icons. This suddenly made computers much easier to use. There was no need to remember a long list of commands. One could just click on an icon.

6. The increase in processing power for mini-computers/mainframes, the invention of PCs and GUIs allowed the concept of client-server computing to be born. The theory behind this is that there is a central computer that provides data to many networked PCs.

7. Finally, the first primitive video conferencing systems were implemented, although they were very slow to use because of the very limited network bandwidth.

This explosion of technology improvements triggered several changes to how Financial Services firms operate:

1. There was a continued increase in the automation of manual processes. This covered many areas such as account openings and insurance liability oversight.

2. The increase in database technology and the associated data analysis software allowed firms to genuinely start to perform analysis on their clients, sales, profits, costs, and so on. (It could be argued that this was the first attempt at data mining with the financial services industry.) Firms could assess their client base to see which ones made their money, which ones cost them money, investigate cross-selling opportunities, and so on. Firms could also investigate their operating costs to see where there were blockages so process improvements could be implemented.

3. There was also an increase in harmonizing standards across the industry. For example, the same message format would be used across the industry for sending money, instructing a foreign exchange trade, and so on. This allowed much easier communication between firms which then helped with the increase of industry infrastructure.

This standardized messaging helped enormously with making payments

1. In 1984, the world's first online shopping took place. Jane Snowball, from Gateshead UK, purchased food from her local supermarket using video technology.
2. In the late 1980s and early 1990s, the Globex trading went live and its standard messaging allowed access to a range of financial assets such as treasuries, foreign exchange, and commodities.
3. In 1986, the UK ATM network LINK went live with 33 banks and building societies which allowed customers of each of the 33 members to withdraw money from any of the members' ATMs. In 1989, LINK merged with the Matrix Network to provide more coverage for customers across the UK.

This standardized message also helped with trading and general market infrastructure, namely:

1. In 1971, the National Association of Securities Dealers Automated Quotation (or NASDAQ) was formed in New York, in the United States, to allow trading across parties.
2. Finally, the convergence of standards also helped with the forming of SWIFT (Society for Worldwide Interbank Financial Telecommunication) which provides a network for financial institutions to send messages to each other in a secure, standardized, and reliable manner. SWIFT covers a wide range of messages such as Cash, Treasury, and Securities updates and movements.

Another interesting development during this period was the growth in firms purchasing software packages. Previously, firms used to develop and support their software in-house or outsource their computing to service bureaux. This was costly and time-consuming. However, with the growing trend of standardization and requirements being similar, it was easier to purchase a package "off the shelf" to meet the need. These were quicker and often cheaper to implement. For example, there were various packages to allow connectively to SWIFT, make global payments, or maintain books and records.

However, having said this, there was also a trend to take standard off-the-shelf packages and bespoke them for each firms' needs. This created further complexity and risk. With hindsight, it would have been better if firms would have changed their ways of working to fit in with the purchased package worked as opposed to enhancing the package to fit in with the way the firm worked.

While the above developments were impressive and provided a large number of benefits to the Financial Services, they caused a variety of problems.

1. Firstly (and as mentioned above), the new technologies only really allowed changes to the inner workings of firms or the general market infrastructure. There was little benefit to the customers.
2. Also, technology infrastructures started to become really "complex." They often consist of different technologies (e.g., mainframes, minis, and PCs), running various packages (covering in-house developed, standard off-the-shelf packages, and bespoke off-the-shelf packages), and a spaghetti of integrations between in-house systems and market infrastructures. This infrastructure needed to be supported and maintained by an expensive staff base covering many different skill sets.
3. Firms were completely reliant on technology to operate which meant any outages or issues could be serious problems. Therefore, firms had to implement controls around their technology to ensure it operated as designed with suitable measures in place in the event of problems. This helped with the rise of formal standards such as ITIL (was Information Technology Infrastructure Library) is a set of detailed best practices covering Service Design, Service Transition, Service Operation, and Continuous Service Improvement.

Also, these technology infrastructures were becoming more and more complex to change. Previously, upgrading a piece of software was a straightforward task but now, because it is integrated with so many other components, it is a risky and challenging exercise that required a large amount of planning, development, testing, and post-implementation support. Again these challenges help with the rise of standards around Release Management.

4. Finally, there is often an issue with social acceptance. Despite the benefits new technology offers, it is not uncommon for certain people to be nervous about using this technology. Therefore, it could take a while for new technology to become socially acceptable. For example, it took several years for ATMs to become popular in the UK.

Stage 3—Customers Are Now Going Online—1995 to 2005

This age provided many exciting developments which (unlike Stages 1 and 2 above) allowed firms to offer functionality, services, products, and so on externally to the end customer to genuinely improve the service and products offered by firms.

Without a doubt, the most noticeable development during this age was the development of the Internet and World Wide Web (or Web). While these two phrases are often used interchangeably, they are different. The Internet is a packet-switching network based on the TCP/IP network protocol. It was originally called APRANET created by the U.S. Department of Defence Advanced Research Project Agency (ARPA) in the 1960s. The World Wide Web is a series of documents identified by a URL (Uniform Resource Locator) which are linked together by a series of hyperlinks and accessed by an application called a Web Browser. The Web runs on top of the Internet.

The emergence of the Internet and the Web was helped by the continuing increase in processing power (remember Moore's Law from earlier), improvement in programming languages (namely HTML and HTTP), web browsers becoming increasingly mainstream, increases in common standards (to help interconnectivity), the increase in Internet search sites, and the increase in network bandwidth from simple dial-up modems to reliable broadband connectivity.

This perfect storm allowed the Internet (or Web) to become mainstream and offer many opportunities to firms, namely:

1. Firms could develop websites that could allow customers to self-service on a 24-hour day 365 days per year basis. The initial websites were no more than "brochure-ware sites" allowing customers and prospects to download literature, find out information, or request details. However, over time, this functionality would expand to cover easily codified functions such as accessing balances, producing statements, opening accounts, closing accounts, trading, and money transfers.

   This provided some benefits to firms as well. By allowing websites to provide self-servicing functionality, it allowed firms to reduce staff levels on call centers or to ensure staff was focused on the functions that cannot be codified, for example: dealing with deaths or very complex client queries.

2. However, there was an interesting development that was not predicted at the time. The Web allowed new more entrepreneurial and aggressive entrants to enter the financial services market by offering new and/or better functionality. This was good for the customer because it created increased and better products and services and products for them. However, it was the first time in many years that there has been a serious challenge to the existing firms within the industry and many of these existing firms were caught "flat-footed" and were slow to react. For example, in 1998, PayPal was launched which offered a new, convenient and flexible method for making payments, and in 1998, the Egg Internet Bank was launched in the UK. It took some of the existing players at the time several years to react to this.

   This entrepreneurial spirit also allowed many other new products to be developed. In 2003, Chip and PIN was introduced in the UK for safer and easier payments, and in 2004, card spending in the UK exceeded cash for the first time.

3. The final perk for this technology was easier communication. The Internet allowed standardized e-mail, video, instant messaging, secure messages, and file transfers between firms. This improved efficiency and reduced costs.

Despite the great benefits and opportunities of the Internet and World Wide Web, they did cause several key issues.

1. The already complex technology infrastructures (see Stage 2) were becoming more and more complex. On the top of the existing stack of different technologies, various supplier/in-house packages, and a mesh of integrations, a mass of new components needed to be added. This covered the infrastructure to support Internet connectivity, technology to support various websites as well as software integration links from the websites to "back systems" for processing requests (such as account opening). This infrastructure needed to be supported and maintained by a costly set of staff covering many different skill sets.

   However, as firms built websites they have opened up their technology infrastructures to the world. This creates a new type of risk called Cyber. This risk typically relates to any outage, disruption, financial loss, or reputation damage caused by a problem with its technology infrastructures. Specifically, this could cover (a) accidental and/or breaches of security, (b) system outages due to system problems or poor design, (c) somebody deliberately trying to access (or hack) into the system, and (d) somebody trying to steal data. Furthermore also because of the 24 hours-per-day nature of the websites then need full resilience and business continuity processing to cover outages. If a website is unavailable then customers cannot access their details. This type of outage is very visible and can damage a firm's reputation. Therefore, firms need to implement controls and checks to manage these types of risks.

   Therefore, the result is that these technology infrastructures are now unbelievably complex and firms must implement processes and governance to manage the technology infrastructure and the risks associated with it. As mentioned earlier, firms are looking to use formal standards such as ITIL to help with this.

Also as mentioned earlier, these technology infrastructures were becoming more and more complex to change. Any change is a complex process and will need to manage carefully. These challenges help with the rise of standards around Release Management.

2. Similar to the point noted under Stage 2 above, there is often an issue with social acceptance. Despite the benefits the Web offers, people are still nervous about using new technology. This was especially common with online servicing because people were nervous about their details being stolen which in turn made them susceptible to fraudulent transactions. Therefore, it does often take a while for new technology to become mainstream.

3. Finally, several clients do not like the loss of personal contact. While they feel the self-servicing over the Web is useful, they will look to speak to a human about their affairs. They feel nervous about providing confidential details to a "screen" without feeling comfortable with what the "screen" is doing with their details. Also, not everyone must have access to the Internet or World Wide Web. Consequently, firms need to ensure they have a personal element to the client servicing.

Stage 4—Customers Are Now Leading the Industry and Going Mobile—2005 Onwards

This stage effectively brings this short history of financial services and its technology up to date.

This stage can be looked at as the logical progression from Stage 3 where client interaction was moved onto the web to where (for this fourth stage) clients are now using a variety of different hand-held, tablets, phones, and smart devices (over the Internet) to access their details. In effect, clients are now carrying a powerful computer in their pocket and they are demanding instant and full-time access to their details. For example, balances, inquiries must be real-time, or payments must be able to be made at the touch of a button. (This growth is commonly known as the Internet-of-Things and is discussed in-depth in Chapter 9.)

This trajectory has been again been supported by increased processing power (again note Moore's Law from earlier), more open standards, better and more efficient programming languages as well as increased network bandwidth (with 4G and 5G providing customers with what seems like instant access to their details).

It has also been supported by new and emerging technology such as Big Data, Natural Language Processes plus many others. (However, the rest of this textbook discusses these so I will not cover them in detail here.)

Finally, it is worth noting that this fourth stage is also being motivated by societal changes driven by other business areas (Amazon, Facebook, Netflix, LinkedIn, etc.) which are not financial services firms in their own right. These businesses have revolutionized the way society operates with people expecting everything online with instructions executed at the "touch of a button." Therefore, financial services need to follow this trend.

This technology capability expansion has provided some changes to how Financial Services firms operate:

1. Firstly and at the most obvious level, several new distribution methods have been created. The existing web channels have been improved significantly but firms have created sophisticated applications (or "apps") for hand-held devices, smartphones, wearables, and tablets. These apps need to provide all the instant functionality demanded by the majority of customers. For example real-time balance inquiries, real-time transactions, and so on.

2. Also, these improvements in technology have allowed new innovative ways to be implemented to support existing needs. One area of particular note relates to payments where there is several new entrants have implemented products to try and improve the entire payments process. These new entrants are either existing technology firms looking to move into financial services or start-ups driving to push innovation. For example, Apple-Pay, Google-Pay, or Smile-to-pay.

3. Further to the above point, the developments in technology have allowed innovations to be implemented. In 2009, the first version of BitCoin was implemented (and this is discussed more in Chapter 11 below). Also, several crowdfunding services have been launched which allow start-ups to obtain funding quickly and directly from investors without having a bank or some other financial firm in the middle.

4. Finally, there has been an increase in standards to the point that the financial services industry can generally say it is open. The new Open Banking standard is a new technology standard that makes it easier to create interaction between banks regarding moving accounts, supporting other providers' products, and so on. The Open Banking standard will make it easier for new entrants to enter the industry. Likewise, the Banking as a Service platform has made it easier for organizations to launch "neo-banks" or digital banks that have emerged based on improving the customer experience.

However, it is now fair to say that for the very first time in its history, the Financial Services industry is being led by the demands of its customers and clients as opposed to a set of large financial firms.

Despite the great benefits and opportunities of hand-held devices, smartphones and tablets, and World Wide Web there are many key issues.

1. For legacy or existing firms, the complex technology infrastructures (discussed in Stages 2 and 3) are becoming more complex to the point that it is hard to comprehend them. They consist of an interconnected set of different technologies, various supplier/in-house packages, a network of integrations, Internet connectivity, technology to support websites (including links to back end systems), and, now, further technology to support hand-held devices, smart phones, and tablets. Apart from the cost, staffing, and governance required to support this, the risk level (especially Cyber Risk) has increased dramatically.

2. While any new entrant will not have the issues that the legacy firms have, they will still need to build a complex technology infrastructure to support their products and clients. They will need to ensure that have the relevant staffing, governance, and risk management controls in place.

3. Consequently, Financial Regulators are now starting to take a real interest in how firms manage, govern, and oversee their complex infrastructures, especially in the areas of operational resilience (i.e., how do firms cope with outages), the management of suppliers (i.e., do firms have sufficient legal contract clauses over suppliers to ensure they perform what they have committed do?), how data is protected

(i.e., to stop data breaches, etc.) and ensuring firms have named individuals who are responsible for all aspects of their business.

While these regulations are still being finalized, it is clear that failure to comply will result in severe penalties such as fines, termination of licenses, and individual criminal prosecutions of named individuals who are at fault.

4. Again similar to the above in Stages 2 and 3, there is always an issue with social acceptance of new technology. Despite the benefits of mobile computing, people are still nervous about using new technology. As noted earlier, this was especially common with online servicing because people were nervous about their details being stolen and therefore making them susceptible to fraudulent transactions. Therefore, it does often take a while for new technology to become mainstream.

5. Also, some individuals and demographic groups are nervous about using new entrants and would prefer to stick to the "tried and tested" firms. This is something new entrants need to manage and overcome.

6. Again as noted in Stages 2 and 3 above, some clients do not like the loss of personal contact. While they may like self-servicing using their phone they would still like to speak to a human about their affairs or at least be comfortable that they can speak to somebody if they want to quickly.

7. Also, not everyone will have access to hand-held devices, smartphones, and tablets, and (per above) some prefer "face-to-face" interaction. Therefore, firms need to ensure they have a personal element to the client servicing. This is particularly true for firms' older customers who are sometimes uncomfortable with technology.

Summary and Wrap Up

The development of financial services has gone hand in hand with the development of technology generally. As technology has grown, it has allowed financial services to expand. However, financial services are always been a keen user of technology and this use has helped drive the development of the technology holistically.

This growth has been driven by several factors; namely (a) improved processing power, (b) better and more appropriate programming languages, (c) better database technologies, (d) improved usability by factors such GIUs, websites, and mobile devices, (e) improved and more widely used standards, (f) the use of software packages, and (g) improved network bandwidth.

This growth has allowed firms and the general financial services market to prosper in several ways, namely:

- It has allowed firms to generate internal efficiencies, offers new functionality, reduce operating costs, and use wider distribution channels (such as the Internet, websites, and mobile).
- It has allowed firms to become more client-centric by developing products, services, and capabilities that genuinely and continuingly meet client and marketplace needs.
- It has also allowed new entrants to enter the market which are looking at new innovative methods for both existing functionality (such as payments) and new functionality (such as crowdfunding). While this is generally good for customers, it can be a threat to existing firms in the industry.

However, this progress does come at some cost around the complexity of technology infrastructures.

- The hardest-hit area is legacy firms that have been in the business for many years. Their infrastructure consists of overlaying layers of interconnecting sets of different technologies, supplier/in-house packages, networks of integrations, Internet connectivity, technology to support websites (including links to back end systems), and, now, further technology to support hand-held devices, smartphones, and tablets. Apart from the cost, staffing, and governance required to support this, the risk levels (particularly around cyber and operational) are high.
  There is also the element of supplier risk because some of the older technology is becoming increasingly difficult to support as the

software developers who developed them are retiring and young
people don't want to train in old tech.

- New entrants to the market will not have this baggage but
  they still need to have appropriate staffing and governance
  in place to support their infrastructures and associated risks.
  However, the challenge for new entrants is establishing
  credibility in the marketplace and with their targeting
  customer base.

Consequently, Financial Regulators are now starting to take a real interest in how firms manage, govern, and oversee their complex infrastructures, especially in the areas of operational resilience (i.e., how do firms cope with outages), the management of suppliers (i.e., do firms have sufficient legal contract clauses over suppliers to ensure they perform what they have committed do?), how data is protected (i.e., to stop data breaches, etc.), and ensuring firms have named individuals who are responsible for all aspects for their business. While these regulations are still being finalized, it is clear that failure to comply will result in severe penalties such as fines, termination of licenses, and individual criminal prosecutions of named individuals. It is also expected that this regulatory scrutiny will continue with the implementation of the emerging technologies discussed in the rest of this book.

Finally, there is an issue around social acceptance of technology changes. Some individuals and demographic groups are slow in taking up new technologies which means firms will need to support this group of clients). Also, some groups are nervous about using new entrants and would prefer to stick to the "tried and tested" firms. This is something new entrants need to manage and overcome.

CHAPTER 4

What Are the Challenges for the Financial Services Industry?

The two previous chapters were very much focused on discussing the structure of the financial services industry and how technology has helped shape the industry. This chapter is very much looking into the future by discussing the ten key challenges that will need to be tackled head-on.

The ten challenges are summarized in Figure 4.1 below and are explored further in this chapter.

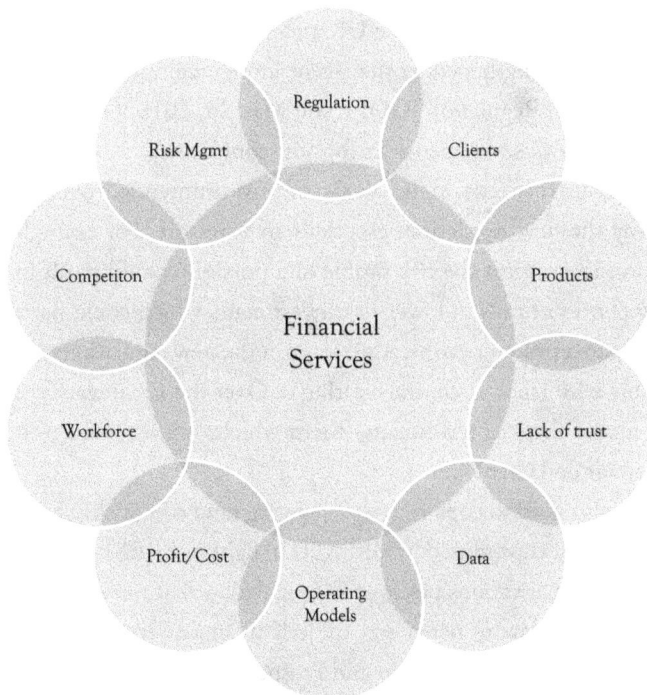

Figure 4.1 Summary of the challenges of impacting the financial services industry

A "Tsunami" of New Complex and
Business-Critical Regulation

Arguably, the most prominent factor at the moment is Regulation or, more specifically, the "tsunami" of new regulations which is inundating the Asset Management industry following the credit crisis of 2008. This wave of new and updated regulation is set to continue for the foreseeable future. This complex set of existing and new global regulations is and will continue to provide many challenges to the industry. For example, increased costs to comply which is squeezing profit margins, an adverse impact on innovation increase complexity.

These challenges are, in turn, forcing the industry to change the way they work. Firms need to review cultures, capital requirements, product development processes, investment strategies, marketing approaches, distribution, their operating model, and associated infrastructures as well developing the ability to complete regulatory returns.

Firms also need to develop new capabilities to comply with data protection regulations covering the ability to collect, retain and process data, and manage information. In the UK and European Union, this area has recently been strengthened by the recent implementation of the General Data Protection Regulation (GDPR) on May 25, 2018. GDPR itself is a complex law with severe penalties for non-compliance.

The industry needs to be aware of any unintended consequences caused by the new regulation, especially to Investors. For example, new regulation to monitor the risk profile of a portfolio could result in firms putting pension funds in lower-risk investments which could harm their long-term investment returns. Also, some of the new regulations are costly to comply with (such as central clearing of Over the-Counter derivatives) which means firms could not use them which, again, could ultimately impact their end client.

Firms also need to cope with the changing (and still unclear at the time of writing) landscape caused by BREXIT. In light of BREXIT, the Government is looking at various pieces of EU regulation that may be removed or modified in UK law to better suit the UK financial services industry; for example: Lord Hill's UK Listings and Prospectus reviews. This may lead to those firms operating in the UK and the EU having to operate two regulatory regimes side by side to accommodate the diverging regulations.

Therefore, it is now essential that firms develop capabilities to ensure they can comply with these regulations. Some commentators have joked by saying the regulation is the biggest growth area within Financial Services.

The Changing Nature of Clients

The second characteristic is the changing nature of clients.

As discussed earlier, the Financial Services industry has a wide range of different types of clients which range from very large multi-billion pound multi-national organizations, using many products, down to individual retail clients who may only have a simple bank account.

However, the dynamics of this group are changing.

Since the credit crisis in 2008, Investors are becoming more knowledgeable and they are focusing their attention on a wider range of activities. For example, performing reviews on the firms' products, usability, and fees. They are also looking for Managers to take a more ethical attitude with their investments (hence the increase in demand for ESG compliant products). Clients are now more willing to change providers on a more regular basis and initiatives such as open banking will enable these changes.

Secondly, the dynamics or the "make-up" of clients are changing. At a global level, life expectancy has risen by 50 percent, the world population has risen and there has been a sharp rise in the ratio of global wealth to income. This means there are more savers, younger savers, older savers, and richer savers. This global change directly impacts the profile of the group. At the lower Retail end of the business, the impact is more obvious because more savers will mean more Retail clients. However, there will be impacts to the higher end because more savers will mean bigger Pension Funds and increased tax revenue which will boost the size of Sovereign Wealth Funds.

Thirdly, clients are taking on more responsibilities for managing their assets and liabilities. A prime example of this is the move from Defined Benefit pension funds in the UK to Defined Contribution funds where the emphasis is on the client to proactively manage investment decisions. Second, there has been an increase in High Net-Worth Individuals and Sovereign Wealth Funds with more diverse agendas and challenging investment goals.

Consequently, the industry needs to understand that the clients' perspective of value is getting tough and it will need to get much smarter at understanding what clients value.

The Changing Nature of Products

There is an also ongoing sea-change in the types of products within the industry. There are a large number of products in the industry that are currently being rationalized into fewer products but with a greater concentration. This change has been driven by the following factors.

Firstly, the increased burden of regulation has resulted in many products being too costly and complex to run. Historically, firms have never really understood the costs behind their products mainly because the margins were large enough that costs always appeared immaterial. However, since the introduction of more regulation the costs and complexity to comply have increased which has resulted in many products being uneconomical.

Secondly, client demands have evolved which means many products do not meet their clients' needs. Using Asset Management as an example; products ranges are moving away from pure alpha equity managed returns to products focused on advice and outcomes balanced against cost and investor liquidity needs. Defined Benefit pension funds nowadays are more interested in having dedicated cash flows to meet pensioner payments (i.e., outcomes) as opposed to having their investments outperform the FTSE-100 by 1 percent each year (i.e., alpha returns). Also, firms are having to develop and offer products that support sustainability and the global trend to tackle climate change.

Finally, firms tended to be distant from their Investors and did not offer any significant personal or customer service. However, firms need to ensure the Product Offers are expanded to provide much better customer service elements going forward.

Lack of Trust in the Industry

The fourth characteristic within the industry is the lack of trust that clients (and the general public) have in the entire industry. There has always been a lack of trust in financial services firms but this trust was destroyed by the Credit Crunch of 2008. The lack of trust has been kept going by a constant associated stream of damaging media stories covering areas such as general incompetence, poor customer service, and undeserved bonuses.

While certain parts of the industry (say Building Societies or Asset Managers) could reasonably argue that they were not part of the cause of the credit crunch, because it was caused by Investment Bankers and their actions, they are deemed "guilty" in the public's eye. Therefore, firms must have sufficient governance and risk capabilities to try and increase trust.

This characteristic can be split into two areas: namely, tangible capabilities and intangible capabilities.

The tangible capabilities are primarily driven by the new regulation currently being implemented. This regulation is forcing firms to implement greater oversight responsibilities, new governance models, and new processes to support decision making, risk management, and transparency. The challenges of implementing this have been discussed in more detail above.

However, the other grouping is intangible capabilities with items such as cultural change, behavior change, and ensuring that no silos exist to stop the flow of data. This area is far more challenging because changing deep-rooted behaviors is a complex task. Firstly, individuals themselves will need to change and then their interactions with other individuals will then need to change. This is an area that the regulators are particularly focusing on.

The Need for Accurate Data

The fifth characteristic of the industry is the need for timely and accurate data. This is essential to all parts of the industry and it could be argued that this is the "blood" of the industry.

Currently, data is required for: understanding client bases, managing the investor's assets, managing distribution channels, completing regulatory returns, cost/profit management, governance processes, product management, and decision making.

Looking forward (and as this book will demonstrate) more data will be required to support future changes such as supporting newer technologies (such as Machine Learning), monitoring climate footprints, and self-servicing plus many others.

Unfortunately, many firms struggle to produce timely and accurate data due to major efficiencies in their operating and technology platforms. This is discussed further below.

Poor Operating and Technology Models

The sixth characteristic of the industry is the constant challenge that operating and technology models have to keep pace with the changing nature of the industry.

Historically, these operating models have been costly to operate, rarely "fit for purpose," and hard to manage. They consist of a complex piecemeal set of duplicate, ineffective, and poorly implemented technology, a variety of in-house manual processes and various third-party outsourced arrangements covering various and duplicate functions. However, the demands of extra regulation, more demanding customers, new product ranges, requirements for online access, and the need for accurate and timely data as well as superior governance processes will place more pressure on these already struggling platforms.

These extra demands will stretch the already struggling capabilities of these operating models because they will be expected to cope with more demands. The result is that various processes and technologies are "bolted" onto the side of the operating model which only increases their "patchwork quilt" nature. It will also start to open up newer risks such as the increased presence of cyber-risk caused by firms "opening up" their operating models to allow external clients online access.

Some firms have looked at various change initiatives to make a step change to improve their operating model. These can range in size from small system upgrades to massive business transformation activities. However, the industry has a poor record in implementing change and many of these change initiatives do not provide the benefits hoped and could make the situation worse or more "cobbled together."

Profit and Cost Pressures

The majority of firms are economic firms as in they need to make a return of some sort (normally a profit). There are a few firms that are non-profit making (such as a pension fund owning the Asset Manager who manages their assets or mutually held building societies who are only responsible to their customers) but these firms will still need to generate sufficient income to cover their operating costs.

However, the constant demands mentioned in this chapter are increasing costs as well as reducing revenue which means managing costs has become more and more challenging.

Changing the Nature of the Workforce

This is a major challenge for the industry and covers three main areas such as (a) increasing workforce and cultural diversity, (b) the impact of COVID-19 and the move to home working, and (c) improving the work-life balance.

Increasing Workforce and Cultural Diversity

It is fair to say the financial services industry had a major image problem that cause blockages around the workforce and cultural diversity.

There was a perception that all people who worked in the industry was "loud-mouthed" arrogant people who worked long hours with the focus on making as much money for themselves as possible often to the detriment of other staff members, other industry participants, and their clients (i.e., the people who they were supposed to be servicing). This perception was often reinforced by the media and some high-profile films during the 1980s. This behavior resulted in extreme risk-taking (or completely ignoring risks). It was very much the case of if the money was coming in then everything is good.

This reckless behavior caused some issues:

- Firstly, there were some cultural "defects" that created massive market risks. For example, money was loaned to individuals who clearly could not pay it back, or complex Credit Default Swaps are created with large exposures that individuals did not fully understand. Once these risks started to crystallize then this caused a chain of reactions which caused the credit crisis of 2008 and almost brought down several financial services firms and severely weakened the entire global economy.

- Secondly and just as importantly, it severely restricted workforce diversity. While it is fair to say that not all people in the industry matched the stereotype listed above, there was a clear perception that all people in the industry were like that. Therefore, as somebody's perception is their reality it did discourage and marginalize certain groups (e.g., females, BAME, LBGT plus others) across the industry. There is a large amount of evidence that diverse workflows produce better outcomes that are good for the firm and customers (i.e., the people who firms are supposed to support).

Therefore, the industry is looking to address this in two main ways:

- Regulators are looking to implement new rules to force firms to change their cultures and ways of working. For example, the UK has recently implemented a new regulation called Senior Managers and Certification Regime (SMCR) which makes individuals responsible for certain aspects of a firm's activity. Failure to comply could result in criminal prosecution. It is hoped that by making individuals responsible then risks will be managed better.
- Secondly, firms are looking to improve diversity across their firms to ensure previously under-represented groups are grown. This involves "carrot" tactics such as encouraging and, if necessary, positive discrimination and well as "stick" tactics where disciplinary measures could be evoked if individuals block diversity.

The Impact of COVID-19 and the Move to Home Working

This is very much a live issue at the time of writing. Speaking from a UK point-of-view, in March 2020, nearly all financial firms had to move to a home or remote working almost overnight. This created some immediate issues that both firms and individuals had to adapt to almost immediately.

Most firms have to split their workforce between the office and remote working. Office working covered functions that could not be done remotely (such as opening bank branches) and these were subject to strict COVID-19 restrictions such as social distancing. All other functions had to move to a remote or home method. Therefore, firms had to adapt their operating model to support remote work. IT technologies are needed to support hundreds, if not thousands, of staff working at home. These changes changed the risk profile of firms with cyber and operational risks becoming more prominent. Furthermore, the management staff had to change to reflect this remote nature with different methods being used for supervision and communication.

There were also impacts on the actual staff. There has been a blur between life and work. People have had to cope with child care arrangements. Individuals have also complained about working longer hours, not being able to switch off from work, social isolation, domestic issues, and other mental health issues.

Having noted these issues, there have been some advantages. Having an operating model split across many locations provides natural Business continuity planning ("BCP") because firms' operations are not completely dependent on a few central locations. Furthermore, some firms are looking to reduce costs by either non-renewing or extending rent on expensive property. Also, staff have enjoyed spending time with their families as well as not having to spend many hours on the daily commute.

As the COVID-19 restrictions have started to relax, firms are now looking at how they can bring their staff "back into the office." While we are still in the early stages, it is safe to say that the working model will be different. It is unlikely that all staff will return to the office. While some staff will have to return to the office full time (e.g., bank branch staff or those who require very specific technology), there will be a hybrid model for others with some working at home for some or all of the time.

Therefore, firms will need to implement the operating model, technology, staff process, and risk mitigation processes to cover this.

Work-Life Balance

There has been a long debate about improving the work-life balance for financial services firms' staff. There is a clear perception that staff works long hours (often with a long commute) which means a poor non-work life (e.g., reduced family and social time). As noted above; in the post-COVID-19 work, firms will likely allow staff to work at home for some or all of the time. This could make some changes to the work-life balance. However, (again as noted above) firms will need to implement the operating model, technology, staff process, and risk mitigation processes to cover this.

New Competitors and Market Entrants

The Financial Services industry has traditionally been dominated by the same set of firms for many years. While the make-up of the firms has changed, it is often caused by existing firms performing mergers, demergers, or take-overs.

In recent years, several genuinely new firms have entered the market. Some struggle with the weighty entry barriers around regulatory compliance, operating models, technology, distribution channels, and costs. Therefore, either these new entrants fail or are taken over by an existing player. Alternatively, our new entrants are boilerplates of existing players. For example, several supermarkets launching investment products but they are effectively distributing products that are supported by existing players.

The growth of technology (i.e., the theme of this book) has allowed new players to enter the market. For example Apple-Pay, Google-Pay, and Cryptocurrencies. Although it could be argued that these entrants are only improving an existing service (e.g., payments) as opposed to offering something completely new, it is important to note that some of these new entrants (e.g., cryptocurrencies) are at higher risk because they are not regulated appropriately.

There are also some less obvious new entrants. For example, some larger Pension Funds (i.e., an Investor) are building capabilities for them to directly manage their assets and to reduce their reliance on external Managers.

However, having a constant flow of new and credible entrants is beneficial to any industry. This is because new entrants will highlight gaps in the market and/or improve existing offerings which will both (a) bring the industry forward and (b) improve the offerings for customers. Also, new entrants ensure existing market players are kept "on their toes" to ensure their offerings are constantly improving which, in turn, is in the interest of customers.

The Need to Manage Risks

There is also a key theme for Firms to manage their risk profile and appetite. This has stemmed from the credit crisis in 2008 where (with hindsight) a large number of firms did not have the correct risk controls in place which meant they have large exposure to risky investments (such as property and Contract Default Swaps).

Risk cover many areas such as operational risk (i.e., errors or problems with the operating model), regulatory risk (i.e., the possibility of purposely or accidentally not complying with regulations), market risk (i.e., the chance of prices and exchange rates changing causing a financial loss), credit risk (i.e., borrowers not paying back money loaned to them or for counterparties not settling trades on time), and cash risk (i.e., running out of cash for day-to-day operations).

Therefore, firms (with the insistence of regulators) now carefully monitor their risk profiles to ensure they are fully understood and controlled.

The cost to the industry of monitoring and management of risk is huge. However, with the regulatory focus on risk and the broadening spectrum of risks to be managed, the cost to the firm of not managing it effectively is even bigger.

CHAPTER 5

Trend 1—Remote Working

Introduction

Traditionally, financial services firms have to operate from offices and branches with very little remote working or working from home. This has been caused by several factors.

- The first one is the obvious need that firms often have customer-facing branches which need staff to support them. It would not be possible to run a bank branch with staff working remotely.
- Secondly, there was a traditional "alpha-male" attitude in financial services where the staff was expected to work long hours in their office to prove their dedication.
- Finally, there was also the popular but very controversial argument that it was "easier" to manage staff if you could "see what they were doing" and people working from home could not be trusted.

Overview of Remote Working

Over the past few years, there has been a general movement to support remote working for two main reasons:

Work-Life Balance

There has been a general cultural change and firms are willing to support remote working for their staff. This has been caused by the general theme of firms trying to improve the work-life balance of their staff allowing them to work different hours to spend more time with family, perhaps care for a sick relative, working hours that are more convenient to the staff member, or even work part-time.

COVID-19

The second driver has been the COVID-19 pandemic which (at the time of writing in winter 2021) is still very much in place and a major worry. When the pandemic arrived in February/March 2020, all firms had to almost instantly move to a remote working environment overnight. This caused several immediate issues:

1. Initially, there was a massive strain on firms operating models and the technology that supports them. Thousands of staff had to suddenly work from home which causes a massive strain on firms' technology with a massive increase in demand for remote networking and conference technology. It also cause issues for staff who had to work from laptops and use their broadband as well as other challenges such as not being able to print off documents.

2. Secondly, the move to remote working caused massive issues for individual staff as well as impacting their mental health.

   - Staff who both worked and had young children had to implement staff-child arrangements such as one parent looking after the children in the morning while the other parent works, and swapping roles in the afternoon. Also, it was not then common for both parents to continue working in the evening to ensure they completed all the work required.

   - Staff suffered from the lack of social contact with many staff (especially those living alone) mentioning they suffered from loneliness. To try and combat these, many firms implemented arrangements where they ensured they spoke to staff who were at risk, at least once a day to ensure they are safe and well. Firms also run ran virtual coffee mornings, informal video conference gatherings, quizzes plus other activities to ensure staff was in constant contact.

- In a similar vein, families and couples have struggled with "living on top of each other" with sharing workspaces and increased tension. This increased domestic and family issues.

3. Firms also needed to look at their employment contracts with their staff, namely

- Do firms need to amend their employment contracts to reflect the fact that staff were working at home now?
- How did the move to working from home impact staff insurance contracts? For example, if a staff member has an accident while working from home then who is at fault?
- Also, firms needed to ensure that their staff complied with the necessary health and safety legislation. This meant firms had to provide laptops, desks, screens, printers, and chairs if the staff members felt they needed it.

4. While there was a general movement to working from home, firms still needed to support the staff who needed to work in the "traditional office." This could cover main areas such as critical staff (e.g., senior management), staff who needed specific technology that could not be deployed remotely (e.g., traders), or staff who perform that cannot be performed remotely (e.g., working in a high street branch of a bank or opening the post).

At the time of writing (winter 2021), firms are starting to look to move staff away from remote working arrangements back toward a return to the "traditional" work in an office arrangement. However, many firms are worried about the risk of this as the pandemic rumbles on and therefore are uncomfortable with a full move back.

Therefore, firms are investigating options to reduce or mitigate this risk. One option is a staggered approach with staff working some days remotely and some days in the office. To reduce the risk even further then this staggered migration will probably be phased to ensure there is no material impact on the operations of the business and the staff well-being. For example, the first phase contains staff who want to return to the office, live locally (and not reliant on public transport), or live on their own and miss the social contact of work. The second phase will contain all other staff.

However, while this approach sounds straight-forward and simple, there are several complications, namely:

1. Many firms operate across different countries and each country has different rules for lockdown as well as different social and cultural norms. Therefore, a return to office approach for England may not be suitable for another country such as Scotland, France, Ireland, or the United States. Consequently, if the firm tries to implement a single policy globally then, at worse, it would not work due to the regional differences, and, at best, it could cause resentment between regions because they feel other regions are being treated differently than themselves.

2. Furthermore, some staff has moved away from where they lived before lockdown. For example, they have not renewed the rent on their flat and moved either back with their parents or in with their partners. Therefore, if these staff are forced to start to return to the office then they will have to spend a large amount of money on long commutes or look to rent (again costly) temporary accommodation local to the office when they need to work there.

3. While firms' offices are clean, very well maintained, and will have some sort of social distancing in place, staff still need to commute into their office to work there. This could mean using public transport such as tram, train, or bus networks. Despite the massive efforts of the transport companies, public transport is often crowded with very little social distancing. This means staff could feel uncomfortable using it at peak hours.

4. Some staff have struggled to work from home, others have enjoyed working from home. It has allowed them to improve their work-life balance, perform more work efficiently, and avoid costly and time-consuming commutes. Furthermore, it could be argued that firms have operated reasonably smoothly remotely for over 18 months, and hence why do we need to return to the office? Therefore, these staff will be keen to continue to work from home as much as possible.

Firms need to have policies in place in case staff refuse to return to the office.

5. Staff mental health also needs to be monitored and looked after. Since people have started to work several months from home then they have worked longer hours which caused stress, family problems, and tiredness. This means the financial services industry (and society in general for that matter) may be only starting to see the effects of the COVID-19 pandemic in terms of physical and mental health and well-being. Many people may think "they are okay" at the moment but problems are being stored up which could explode any time soon.

Remote Working Is Here to Stay

Regardless of the points made above, it is fair to say that remote working is here to say. This can be evidenced by a study completed in summer 2021 and published by City-AM in July 2021 where (a) 24 percent of the UK financial services workforce of ~1,000,000 people would like to work at home permanently and (b) 69 percent would like to work from the office a maximum of two days per week. While statistics are not available for other jurisdictions (such as the United States or other parts of Europe), it is safe to assume that there will be a similar trend.

This means that firms and their staff will need to implement changes and arrangements to ensure they can cope with this change in working patterns.

Challenges of Remote Working

Reliance on Staff Infrastructure

To operate, firms will be reliant on their staff's infrastructure. This will cover many areas.

Initially, some sort of remote device (e.g., PC, Laptop, tablet, or smartphone) is required. While the firm can provide a laptop, this is not always the case. If so, the staff member will need to provide their device and ensure its operating system and security software (such as virus protection) are kept up-to-date. Besides, there is a risk that hackers could access the device. There is also a physical issue because devices can be damaged, left on public transport, or the battery could go flat which again increases the risk for the firm.

In addition, the staff member will need to ensure that they have access to Wi-Fi to allow them to access the firm's infrastructure. Wi-Fi can be expensive and, in certain cases, unreliable and insecure. This unreliability will cause day-to-day operational issues and risks for firms because staff will lose connection to the network and consequently cannot perform their job. The lack of security causes cyber risks because confidential data could be stolen by hackers.

Finally, the staff member will need to ensure there is some sort of working area that they can use. Apart from the device mentioned above, there needs to be a desk, screen, printer, chairs, and so on. However, some firms are happy to provide this if required.

An Infrastructure to Support Remote Working Is Needed

This area contains three parts. The first part is ensuring that staff can access the firm's network remotely from their device. The second and third parts are ensuring that once staff have accessed it then they have sufficient communication tools and their applications continue to operate as previously.

Ensuring Staff Can Access the Firm's Network Remotely Using Their Device

Firms will need to implement an infrastructure that will allow staff to securely, easily, and with reliability access the network from the local PC, laptop, tablet, or smartphone. There is a wide range of remote access applications, of which, some require actual applications to be installed whereas others can be accessed by using an Internet browser.

However, three key factors need to be met:

1. Firstly, the application needs to be easy to use. Firms do not want their staff spending hours each day trying to connect to the service.

2. Secondly, the applications need to have good performance. Again, firms do not want their staff to spend (what will seem like) hours for the system to load e-mails or run applications. Using slow applications can be very stressful.

3. Finally, the application needs to be secure with encryption and other security features.

Communication Tools

With remote working, staff will need effective and easy-to-use tools to ensure there is a flow of information to allow them to perform their jobs. These tools will cover remote collaboration, e-mails, instant messaging, conference calls, document sharing, and voice calls. Furthermore, it will be necessary to ensure these tools can communicate with, not just in-house colleagues, but external parties such as suppliers, customers, regulators, and other industry participants.

There are a variety of platforms and systems available and they are all generally very good for supporting remote working. However, firms must decide on a single set of tools to use to avoid confusion, maximize adoption, and ensure consistency. However, firms also need to ensure they are happy with the security features of these systems.

Ensuring Applications Continue to Operate as Previously

As well as being able to access the firm's infrastructure and communicate with required parties, staff working remotely must be able to access the applications that they need to perform their day-to-day jobs.

This has posed several challenges:

1. Some applications (like trading platforms or cash payment portals) require specific hardware which required firms to either (a) install this hardware remotely and/or (b) ensure the staff who operate this travel into the office to use it.

2. Secondly, some applications have specific licenses which detail the location where the application can be used. These locations are typ-

ically the firms' offices and not remote locations such as staff home addresses. To address this problem firms had to both try and amend the user licenses to allow remote users or make arrangements for the staff who use the application to travel into the office.

3. Finally, arrangements need to be put into place to ensure that upgrades can be performed remotely with minimal impact on staff.

Enhanced Cyber Policies and Cyber Monitoring

As discussed above, remote working caused a large number of cyber issues and risks.

Therefore, firms need to ensure their cyber policies around are updated (around password rules, applying updates to home devices, rules around Wi-Fi Security, and sharing of files). These policies will need to be communicated to all staff working remotely to ensure (a) they fully understand why the policies are required, (b) staff fully understand what they need to do to comply with the policies, and (c) fully understand what the implications are if they do not comply with the policies such as disciplinary action.

Firms will also need to implement support processes to allow staff to raise questions or queries if they do not understand the policy or are having challenges with compliance with them. For example, a staff member is struggling to implement a security upgrade on their home device.

Finally, firms will then need to implement controls and oversight to ensure the firm is complying with its policies. Any breaches will need to be trapped, escalated, and managed accordingly.

Enhanced Staff Contracts and Human Resource (HR) Policies

Firms will need to ensure they update their staff employment contracts and support HR policies to reflect remote working. This could cover a range of areas such as follows:

- Changing working locations (to reflect that staff are working remotely, in the office, or a hybrid of both).
- Changing working hours (especially if staff have to work different hours to look after children and family).

- Insurance implications—for example, if a staff member has an accident while working from home then who is at fault?
- Grievance policies—that is, how do they work remotely? Or does remote working create any new type of risk?
- Maternity/Paternity—that is, how does it work remotely?
- Poor staff performance—that is, who is responsible for monitoring staff performance remotely? How does this work in practice? Does this create any additional risks for firms?
- Disciplinary/Termination of contract—that is, how does it work remotely? Or does remote working create any new type of risk?
- Sickness—that is, how does it work remotely? Or does remote working create any new type of risk? How do firms genuinely know that a member of staff is sick?
- Redundancy—that is, how does it work remotely? Or does remote working create any new type of risk?
- Recruitment—that is, how does it work remotely? Or does remote working create any new type of risk?
- Desk booking—that is, when staff working in the office need a desk to work in, will they be given a dedicated desk or will they "hot desk?" Regardless of approach then support policies and procedures will be required.

Look After Staff and Their Well-being

Firms need to implement arrangements to ensure they take special steps to look after staff well-being. This could include staff living on their own, staff who are single parents, or staff who are carers for an ill member of their family. These arrangements could be just regular "check-ins" to ensure they are well or something more permanent arrange like allowing them more time off to support them.

Also, some firms are looking to use staff well-being as a staff benefit to try and either create existing staff or recruit new staff.

Enhanced Remote Technology Support Model

With staff working remotely and working longer hours, the technology support model needs to be enhanced to cater to this.

This will involve support teams working long hours to ensure applications are supported as and when required. While the majority of problems can be addressed remotely, there could be problems that require the support team to have "hands-on access to the device." Therefore, a process will need to be implemented to allow staff members to bring their devices into the office to allow support staff to access them.

In a similar vein to the above, remote staff may have hardware issues that may require hardware to the replaced. Therefore, a process will need to be implemented to allow new or replacement hardware to be sent to the staff's remote location.

Enhanced Business Continuity Planning (BCP)

Traditionally, BCP was focused on supporting the outage of an office (say due to a flood) or an application (say due to hardware problems). BCP arrangements could be "cold" (where there is a standby in place which is implemented if the prime service failures), "warm" (where there is a standby that is almost ready to go in the event of a failure in the prime location), or "live" (where the standby solution is already running and will continue to operate if the prime location fails).

However, with remote working, there are two major differences:

Firstly, a firm's location is not a single set of offices as previously but a single set of offices now supported by many remote locations which are typically staff home locations. Therefore, BCP arrangements need to cater for what happens if a member of staff cannot work because of problems with their home device, problems with their Wi-Fi, problems with their Internet provider or some problem with their house (such as a power cut). Firms need to ensure that work can be transferred quickly and smoothly to other team members.

Secondly, firms need to ensure that the infrastructure that staff use to access the firm's network remotely has sufficient BCP in place. If there was a significant failure in this then staff may not be able to access the firm's technology and the firm may not be able to operate. Therefore, firms need to ensure this infrastructure is sufficiently robust with cold, warm, or hot BCP arrangements in place. Furthermore, firms may need to have doomsday plans to bring staff quickly into the office in the event of massive failure.

Business Processes May Need to Change

As part of the migration to remote working then firms may need to change their day-to-day operating processes to cope with remote working. For example, if the processes involve daily meetings then these will need to be held electronically or if the process involved passing paper around then these will need to be replaced by exchanging electronic documents.

The result is that this creates more change and associated risks.

Remote Working Will Cost Firms (At Least in the Short-Term)

Implementing the remote working infrastructure is costly. New technology needs to be implemented, BCP arrangements need updating, business processes need changing, and so on. This amount of change will cost firms in the short term. However, longer-term, if firms have a large percentage of their staff working remotely then they may be able to reduce office space which will result in a decrease in costs.

Future Challenges

Table 5.1 Future challenges for remote working

Area	Details
Increased regulations	The impact is neutral at the moment. There has been no new regulation triggered specifically by the move to remote working. New regulations may appear in the next few years if remote working does become the norm. However (having said this), there is a certain amount of existing regulation in place which impacts these areas. • Regulators are looking to implement new regulations around ensuring firms' operating infrastructures are fully understood, robust and secure. As remote working is now part of firms' operating infrastructures then this area will be covered. • However, there is existing regulation about cyber-security which is increased by remote working. • Finally, there is employment legislation across most countries that stresses that firms have a duty of care to look after the well-being of their staff. Again this area will be impacted by remote working.

(Continued)

Table 5.1 *(Continued)*

Changing nature of clients	The impact is neutral at the moment. Remote working does not impact this future challenge apart from that firms need a working remote infrastructure to support their clients.
Evolution of products	The impact is neutral at the moment. Remote working does not impact this apart from that firms need a working remote infrastructure to support their range of products.
Lack of trust	The impact is neutral at the moment. Again remote working does not impact this area, although it could be argued that allowing staff to work remotely gives the perception that firms are nicer places to work and therefore increases trust in the industry from an employee point of view.
Accurate data	The impact is neutral at the moment. Remote working does not impact this apart from that firms need a working remote infrastructure to provide and support the data required to run their day-to-day operations.
Poor operating and technology models	This area is impacted negatively in a material manner. Firms' operating models are already complex and overlaying the technology challenges, the reliance of staff, cyber risks, HR issues, remote support, more challenging BCP, and new business processes only make this area more challenging.
Profitability/Cost drivers	This area is impacted negatively in the short term but it could be positive to firms in the longer term. Costs will be impacted by the growth of remote work although the long-term impact is unclear. Implementing the remote working infrastructure is costly. New technology needs to be implemented, BCP arrangements need updating, business processes need changing, and so on. However, longer-term, if firms have a large percentage of their staff working remotely then they may be able to reduce office space which will result in a decrease in costs.
Changing nature of the workforce	Remote working does impact the workforce in both beneficial and negative ways. For some individuals remote working is good. It provides them with a better work-life balance and flexibility. If these staff are forced to work in the office then they could look to move to change roles. Some firms may look to offer remote working as an incentive to join a firm. However, for staff, it has caused material issues around loneliness and domestic issues. These staff could be happy to work in the office.
New competition and replacements	There is no impact to this challenge apart from (as mentioned in "Changing Nature of Workforce") that some firms may promote the benefits of remote working as a "carrot" to recruit staff.

Risk profile	Remote working has dramatically increased the risk profile of risks. The reliance of staff to provide infrastructure, technology support remote working, new policies, process changes, and extended BCP arrangements creates more complexity which in turn creates more risk.
	This risk level could be increased further if/once the regulator starts to implement tighter regulations around remote working.
	Therefore, firms need to implement enhanced risk controls and monitoring to ensure any problems are identified early so they can be managed.

Case Study

The firm in question is a UK-based Investment Manager albeit with many remote sales offices spread around the UK and mainland Europe.

When COVID-19 was starting to become a real risk then this firm started to move key functions (such as portfolio management and trading) to contingency arrangements. In effect, the workforce was split into three groups and spread across the main office, the backup office, and working from home. The theory was that if the main and/or backup office were lost then the business could continue to operate by the staff working at home. However, as the COVID-19 situation became more serious, more staff were moved away from the main and backup office to working at home. The only staff who remained in the main office were those who needed specialist technology (such as trading portals). In parallel, all non-key staff was asked to prepare to work from home. This involved staff taking home laptops and ensuring they could log on remotely as well as ensuring any process changes could be implemented quickly.

Once the UK government called for the national lockdown (in March 2020), all key staff were told to work from home and the only key staff who needed to come into the office were those who needed specialist technology. Strict social distancing was implemented across all offices. While the firm had offices outside the UK, it was decided to implement these changes across all offices for consistency and ease of management.

During the COVID-19 lockdown, the firm implemented a large amount of staff support. This covered helplines, ensuring daily calls were held with all staff and regular checks on staff well-being. In addition, the firm provided laptops, printers, desks, and so on to staff who needed them. Furthermore, the firm enhanced the remote working technology to make it as robust and reliable as possible.

The firm is now planning the return to the office. All staff will work a hybrid model with some days in the office and some days working remotely. Their plan is a three-phased approach with volunteers to return to the office first, followed by key staff and then all remaining staff. The office layout has been changed to allow social distancing and a system has been implemented for hot desk booking. The firm has not set a specific timetable because they do not want staff to feel that they are not being rushed back into the office. However, they would like the return to the office to be completed by end-February 2022.

However, many issues need to be addressed. Firstly, different countries have different national lockdowns in place, so, while the firm is trying to create a single policy, they are mindful that these differences need to cater for. There are also some issues where some staff are either uncomfortable about returning (due to having to use public transport) or just flatly refusing to return. These are being dealt with on an individual basis.

Summary

The move to a remote working model has been gathering pace for a while and this trajectory has dramatically increased since the COVID-19 pandemic appeared in early 2020. For the earlier example above, 24 percent of the UK's ~1,000,000 employees want to work at home full-time with another 69 percent only wanting to work in the office a maximum of two days per week.

While some people have welcomed this move (due to an improved work-life balance), there are many downsides that firms need to be aware of and address.

Firstly, staff (especially those who are alone, at risk of domestic issues, or suffering from mental illnesses) do not like working remotely. They would prefer to work in the office. Firms must recognize this and implement suitable controls.

Secondly, the corporate risks increase with remote working due to the reliance on staff infrastructure, more complex operating models (due to remote working, enhanced BCP arrangements, and business process changes) as well as the new or extended support functions required.

Finally, these changes come with an increase in costs; however, there is a possibility that if firms can reduce office space and associated overheads then cost savings could be made.

CHAPTER 6

Trend 2—Self-Servicing

Introduction

Self-servicing has had several different definitions which can create a certain amount of confusion. However for this book, self-servicing has been defined as follows:

> A situation where the customer performs all parts of activity (such as opening an account or performing a transfer) without any human contact with the firm that supports the client.
>
> This activity will be performed by using a website, a mobile device, an automated telephone line, etc.

What Has Triggered the Growth in Self-Servicing?

Over the last 20 years, the nature of clients who use financial services products has changed dramatically; namely:

1. The number of customers holding financial services products has increased. Previously not everyone used to hold products. However, nowadays, most people (in the Western world at least) hold several products such as bank accounts, investments, pensions, insurance, and others.
2. The range of complexity of customers and their servicing needs has increased. This can range from retail clients who hold one or two simple products with simple service needs to large institutional clients who will hold many complex and bespoke products with far more complex servicing demands.

3. Customers now require access to their products 24 hours a day for 365 days a year. They want updates in real-time (such as cash movements) and they want to perform an activity (such as opening an account) instantly. Customers are not happy to wait until a branch opens or wait until an e-mail or letter is responded to.

These changes in client needs could not be supported by the traditional customer models of bricks and mortar branches opening 9 a.m. to 5 p.m. Mondays to Fridays. Therefore, firms have had to develop self-servicing platforms to meet these challenges.

These self-servicing platforms consist of a set of applications, websites, and automated telephone systems that allow customers to perform all servicing activities themselves immediately without any human involvement from the firm. These platforms are supported by back-end technology enhancements that ensure all updates are processed as soon as the client submits them.

This movement to self-servicing has also been aided by the general advancement of technology, which has provided the necessary capabilities to allow these platforms to be developed. Namely:

1. Increasing processing power and better programming languages have allowed firms to develop more complex and advanced applications.
2. Improved networking (in particular around 4G and 5G) have allowed much quicker connectively and helped provide customers with "instant" access to their products.
3. An increase in open standards across the financial services industry has allowed different providers to link their systems together. For example, because banks use shared standards for transferring money then it makes it much easier to develop systems to allow cross-bank transfers.
4. Other new emerging technologies (such as Nature Language Process (see Chapter 10)) and Big Data (see Chapter 13) have also provided key components that allow self-servicing applications to be implemented.

While self-servicing was driven by customer demands, it has also provided benefits to the firms themselves. Namely:

1. It allowed firms to support an increased number of more complex clients without an associated increase in staffing levels, branches, and costs. These costs can then be passed onto customers as lower fees. (Although it must be noted that a large upfront effort and spend is required to build the self-servicing platform).
2. As self-servicing transactions are being processed via pre-defined codified rules then this allows much better consistency, controls, and governance around activity.
3. Using pre-defined codified rules also allows consistent and more accurate data on customer activity to be gathered. This data can then be used to improve customer service and allow firms to understand customer behaviors which will, in turn, allow (a) new products to be developed and (b) firms to look to cross-sell other products to their clients.

It could also be argued that COVID-19 has helped push the move to self-servicing. During the various lock-downs, customers could not travel to banks or branches to complete an activity and they were forced to use self-servicing platforms. Once they have used the platform then they see their benefits and then continue to use them going forward.

These points can be illustrated by Deloitte's "Realizing the digital promise" report published in 2020 which stated that 35 percent of various banks' customers increased their use of online banking during the pandemic.

Finally, there is an interesting effect of self-servicing in that it has allowed new entrants to enter the marketplace. New financial services firms can set themselves up entirely online reasonably quickly and they do not have the "baggage" of supporting a set of "bricks-and-mortar" branches and offices. This has allowed many new innovative, better and cheaper products to be offered to the benefit of customers. Although these new entrants could mean that existing firms lose market share.

The Uses of Self-Servicing With the Financial Services Industry

In theory, any activity could be automated via self-servicing but typically the best functions are those that can be easily codified into a set of business rules which can then be converted into a computer program. The most common uses are as follows:

Pre-Sales Activity

Pre-sales activity has been available for many years. Websites have had business rules to direct customers and prospects to relevant products so they can download brochures, application forms, and other documents as required. Nevertheless, this offering is somewhat crude and can often be confusing to the customer or prospect.

However self-service has taken this to a far more advanced level. Firms have now built advice or recommendation engines that model a client's needs (e.g., insurance, pensions, savings), their risk appetite (e.g., high or low risk), the demographic profile (e.g., age or life stage) plus many other variables. This modeling can then be used to generate product suggestions and possible recommendations. If the customer is happy with the recommendation then they can be moved to the open account function straight away. The entire process could be completed very quickly.

Account Opening

Self-servicing has allowed the account opening process for most products (such as retail bank accounts, savings products, insurance arrangements, or investments) to be automated. This is because they follow a clear pre-defined set of business rules with a non-negotiable contract. The prospective customer can enter their details, the system can then automatically perform any checks required (such as know-your-customer, credit checks, investment limits, and others), and if everything is successful then the account can be opened and the new customer can then immediately be sent a confirmation with any log on details. This entire process can be completed in several minutes. If there are any issues then the account opening request could be paused and a request would be passed to either a Chabot (see Chapter 8) or a "real" human to investigate.

(For the more complex products and larger institutional clients, the account opening process will follow the more traditional route of filling in a paper application. This is because of the complexity ofthese clients and products, and also because bespoke contracts may be required.)

Live Customer Servicing

A wide range of live customer servicing activities can be performed. For example, providing balances, performing transfers, updating personal details, and fixing logging-in issues. Also, some firms are looking to address other servicing requests by using intelligent Chabot (see Chapter 8) which will try and understand the servicing request and then complete any action required.

Using Data Collected for Customer Improvements and Cross-Selling of Products

As all activity is being performed via a system, all customer behaviors can be recorded consistently and fully. This provides a rich source of data that can then be used for many purposes.

Firstly, any problems or efficiencies with the self-servicing tool can be addressed and improved. For example, making the account opening process easier and simpler to use.

Secondly, it is possible to determine what products customers are interested in so either (a) existing products can be enhanced or (b) completely new products can be developed to meet these needs.

Finally, it is possible to model clients to determine what product cross-selling opportunities are possible. For example, if a customer is looking to open a car loan account then perhaps the firm could look to cross-sell them car insurance at the same time.

Challenges of Self-Servicing

Implementing Self-Servicing Is a Firmwide Change and Needs a Clear Business Reason for Implementation

It is important to remember that implementing self-servicing is a massive undertaking and it will impact all areas of a firm. Technology teams will need to build the technology, operations will need to run the platform, human resources will need to manage the impact on staff jobs, and so on.

So before starting the implementation, the firm must have a clear business reason for implementation that is linked to the firm's strategy. This reason can be something like cost reduction, customer servicing improvements, or keeping up with the competition. Please see Appendix B for a list of the factors to be covered by a Business Case.

Also, the relevant representation must be involved across the business in the project. Self-servicing is not just a technology project.

Finally (and this is discussed in more detail below), when a firm implements self-servicing functionality then it is effectively opening up the inner workings of a firm's operating model. Therefore, if a firm has any major issues with its operating model (such as poor client data, inefficient technology, or poor internal processes) then these issues will become very visible to the customers using the self-servicing functionality. Many firms (not just financial services firms) have had some problems implementing self-servicing which has been caused by internal operating model issues. This has not just resulted in issues for their clients but has resulted in negative media attention and reputational impacts which have taken a while to recover from.

Be Pragmatic About What Functions Will Be Included and Build a Phased Implementation Plan

It is important to be pragmatic about what functions can be included for self-servicing and then ensure these functions are implemented safely and steadily. If inappropriate functions are included and/or the implementation is rushed then it will cause problems that will not just impact customers but could cause reputational damage that could take a long while to recover from.

The best functions to be included are those functions that are easily codified into a set of standard business rules. For example, opening an account, closing an account, performing a transfer, updating personal details, or providing balance updates. For the functions that cannot be included then a manual process will be required. This is discussed under "The uses of Self-Servicing with the Financial Services Industry" (see above). Once a set of functions has been created then it needs to be incorporated into an implementation plan. There are no hard and fast rules for defining this plan but typically they will be ordered in priority of those that give the best customer benefits and also provide the biggest cost savings for the firm. This will ensure that both the customers and the firm receive early benefits.

When the functions are being implemented then this process must not be rushed. To minimize the risk of problems then an initial set of functions should be implemented first. These functions can then be monitored to ensure they are working as planning. If problems are encountered then they can be fixed quickly. Once the firm is happy that these are working satisfactorily then further functions (say account opening) can be rolled out. This phased approach can continue until all functions are live.

However, if all functions are implemented at once in a big bang approach and problems were encountered then it would cause immediate business disruption which will impact clients in a bad way.

Ensure Client Data Is Clean and Accurate Before Starting the Rollout

Self-servicing needs clean and accurate data to work effectively. If client data is incorrect (say the home address or full name is wrong, or the customer cannot see all their products) then customers will lose confidence in the system and either not use it or take their business elsewhere.

However, firms have struggled for years with ensuring client data is clean and accurate. This is for the following reasons:

- Client data is often spread across different internal product systems (say one for banking and another for credit cards) with little or no links between them.

- Also, the data for the same actual client spread across these product systems is often inconsistent. For example, one product system (say loan) may have the full name of a client whereas another product system (say bank a/c or savings) may just have their initials and surname. The simple diagram below illustrates this.

Product System - Loan	Product System – Bank A/c	Product System – Savings
Mr J Bloggs	Mr Joseph Bloggs	Mr Joe Bloggs

Figure 6.1 Product system split of clients

Therefore, before looking to implement self-servicing, all data must be cleansed, all data must be consistent across all product systems, and a customer-centric view is created which links all client's products together. This will provide a solid platform on which self-servicing can be built upon.

Unfortunately, this is a very challenging and expensive task. But several third-party providers are very competent in cleansing data and linking client data across different data sets. The process typically works as follows:

1. A full extract of the client data from all the different product systems is created and sent to the third party with a list of data formatting rules. These data formatting rules could cover date formats, address formats, and so on.
2. The third-party firm will then review all the different product client data against the formatting rules and update the data as required. For example, date formats are changed, address formats are updated, and so on.

   The third-party will also cross-check the different product client data sets to determine whether the same client appears on more than one product system. In effect, this is creating a customer-centric view of all clients and their products. There are different ways that cross-checking can be performed but typically they are on client name, address, date-of-birth, and tax identification number.

3. The updated product client data can then be uploaded into the respective product systems. This will ensure all client data is clean and consistent across all product systems.

4. The list of clients who exist across more than one product system can be used to create the client-centric view, which will link all clients and their products. This single view can be used when presenting self-servicing functionality to clients. See below.

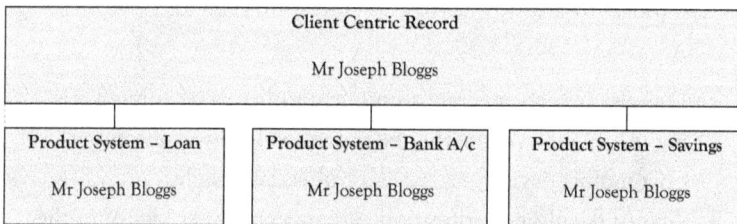

Client Centric Record
Mr Joseph Bloggs

Product System – Loan	Product System – Bank A/c	Product System – Savings
Mr Joseph Bloggs	Mr Joseph Bloggs	Mr Joseph Bloggs

Figure 6.2 Client-centric view of clients

As mentioned earlier, cleansing data is a challenging and expensive task so it is important that once the data is cleaned then processes are put in place to ensure the new standards are maintained. Therefore, automated data feeds will need to be implemented so that when an item of client data is amended or added on one of the product systems then it is replicated immediately on the client-centric record.

Design and Build-In Security Capabilities From the Start

Because self-servicing is being provided over the Internet, implementing suitable and robust security capability is essential. Without this the firm and its clients are at risk of data breaches, fraud, and other criminal activity. This will result in financial loss, reputational damage, and even possible criminal prosecution if the firm has been negligent.

It is also important that security measures are designed and built into the solution from the start. There are various self-servicing projects which have encountered delays, cost overspends, and other issues because they did not include security at the start and a large amount of rework was required to incorporate them.

The key point to remember is that fraudsters and criminals always appear to be one step ahead of everyone so it is important that even when the self-servicing system is live then the security arrangements are constantly reviewed and updated if required.

Traditionally, usernames and passwords have been used but these are not secure. Usernames can be guessed. People often struggle to remember long passwords so either they use the same password for different systems, use memorable names, or write them down. However, there is a general trend to move toward two-factor authentication such as:

- Dongles (which generate a unique number to be entered at log in). Dongles can either be generated by an application on a mobile device or a specialist physical dongle.
- Text or telephone verification. When a customer logs onto the system then either a text message is sent to their telephone or their telephone is called to confirm that it is the client who is trying to log on.
- Location checking where the system will prompt warnings if a customer's account is being accessed from a different location or device. The customer will be asked to confirm that it is the client who is trying to log on before proceeding.

  However, it is important to note that while the above help increases security and reduce the chance of fraud, they do make the platform less pleasant to use.

Design and Build-In Business Continuity Plan (BCP) Capabilities From the Start

It is important to remember that once a self-servicing platform is in place then a firm is completely reliant on it. If there are issues that cause problems or outages then effectively the firm's business will not be able to operate fully which will impact clients badly as well as damaging the firm's reputation. If the problems are significant or constant then the regulator may want to investigate.

The range of outages would cover technology (such as hardware issues, application outages, or network loss) and support functions (such as building outages or power cuts). Therefore, all risks that could cause outages are identified and remedial BCP plans must be designed as part of the implementation. This could involve implementing multiple network links, running multiple versions of applications, or spreading the support functions across several offices.

There are various self-servicing projects which have encountered delays, cost overspends, and other issues because they did not include BCP arrangements at the start and a large amount of rework was required to incorporate them.

Design and Build a Useable Front End for the Customer

Strangely, this is the most important part of implementing self-servicing for customers.

The front-end is the part of the self-servicing platform which the client (or outside world) sees and uses. It will contain various applications for tablets and other mobile devices plus websites and automated telephone services. If the front-end is implemented poorly and not fit-for-use then the customers will not use it and the entire implementation will have failed regardless of how well everything else was implemented.

Therefore, two key considerations from the customer point-of-view must be met:

1. Firstly, the front-end must work for the customer. In other words, it must correctly and consistently perform what it is supposed to do. This covers interacting with the customer as well as integrating with the back-end systems (see "Design and build secure, reliable, and robust integration with back-end systems" (below)). For example, if the front-end is to open an account then it must correctly gather all data, correctly display any errors/messages and correctly pass an update to/from the back end system.

2. Secondly, the front-end must be useable and easy to operate. This just does not cover navigating around the application but ensuring there is suitable online help (such as frequently asked questions, wizards, and Chat-Bots) and it can cope with problems (such as logging in) on its own. If the application is hard to use (regardless of whether it works or not) then the customers will not use it.

However, there are some implications for firms themselves.

- To ensure there is maximum uptake of the self-servicing product then firms will need to ensure it is supported by as many devices as possible (such as tablets, PCs, and phones). Each of these could be running different operating systems and different versions of these operating systems.
- Also, customers could be running different browsers and again different versions of these browsers.

Therefore, all of these combinations will need to be supported which means the different versions of the self-servicing front-end will have to be developed and supported. This is an overhead cost for the firms.

Design and Build Secure, Reliable, and Robust Integration With Back-End Systems

While designing and building a useable application for the customer (see "Design and build a useable 'front end' for the customer" (see above)) is the most important part of the implementation, it can be argued that this area is the most complex and challenging.

At a simple level, many near-instant integrations will need to be developed that will link the front-end used by the customers to the back-end systems to ensure the functionality works. For example, if there is functionality on the front-end to transfer money from one account to another then the client application should be able to pass some sort of messaging to the back-end systems to instruct them to move the money and then receive back sort type of notification confirming that the movement has been made or not.

However, implementing this integration is far from easy for nearly all firms.

As mentioned previously, most firms employ a range of different systems to support their operating model. Each of these systems covers a range of different purposes. For example, some support products (such as loans or investments), and others provide more generic functionality like payments (which in turn will need to integrate with external services such as payment gateways). Also, there is often a range of different technologies used. Additionally, each of the systems has its method for automatically loading data into and extracting data from. Finally, some of the systems are supported by in-house teams whereas others are supported by third-party vendors.

To try and work around some of this complexity the firms will often implement some sort of middleware technology that sits between the customer-facing front-end and the internal back-end systems. The middleware acts as a buffer where it will receive requests from the customer front-end, validate them, reformat them, route them to the relevant back-end system for processing, receive a resource from the back-end system, and then finally send it back to originating customer application. The client-centric view described earlier under "Live Customer Servicing" will assist with this.

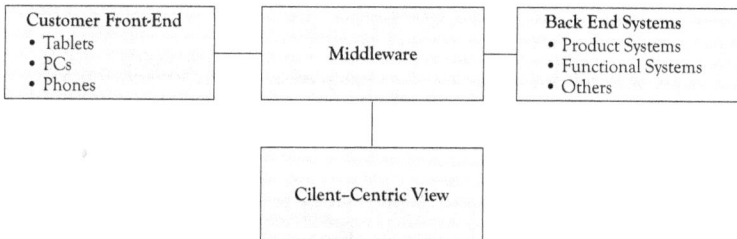

Figure 6.3 Client-centric view of technology

Design and Build a Support Model Around the Self-Servicing Platform

While most of the focus has been around the technology for the platform (such as building the applications for the customers, building in security, and integration with back-end systems), there must be a "human" support model around this technology.

This support model needs to cover many aspects:

1. While the purpose of self-servicing is to remove the amount of human contact and automate all activity, there is still a need to provide some sort of human contact that customers can speak to. This is to cover many areas.

   - Firstly, while the self-servicing functionality is being rolled out then some activity will still need to be done via human contact (although this will reduce as the rollout progresses).
     o Also, there will always be some functions that cannot be codified and included on the self-servicing platform. For example: dealing with customer deaths, legal issues, loan defaults, and so on.
     o Finally, there will always be customers who would be uncomfortable or unable to use the self-servicing platform. They would rather speak to a human to perform an activity. If they could not do this then they would probably close their accounts and it could also generate some publicity for the firm.

2. Sufficient staff will need to be in place to support the technology that underpins the self-servicing platform. This covers:

   - Immediately addressing issues with the various client applications, integrations with the back-end systems, and so on.
   - Reviewing the usage of the applications to allow improvements to the application to be made and to provide data on usage which can be used for product development and cross-sell opportunities.
   - Performing ad-hoc maintenance such as upgrades (say to operate systems or database systems), performing BCP tests, and performing security checks.
   - Implementing improvements to the platform. For example, new functionality, improving existing functionality, updating help screens, and rolling out the platform to new devices.

Future Challenges

Table 6.1 Future challenges for self-servicing

Area	Details
Increased regulations	The impact on these areas is neutral at the moment. The prime reason that regulators exist is to ensure that consumers are protected. Therefore, anything that conflicts with this will grab their attention. While there is no specific regulation in place yet around self-servicing, regulators will want to ensure that customers genuinely benefit from its implementation (and it is not only being implemented for the convenience and financial benefit of firms), all functionality is fit-for-purpose (especially around areas such as advice), it complies with existing regulation and the overall operating model is resilient. If the regulators do become uncomfortable then they may implement new regulations.
Changing nature of clients	The impact on these areas is positive. If self-servicing is implemented properly and correctly then it will benefit clients. It will offer real-time servicing, quicker access to products, and a wide of hours of service. This movement has also been supported by the COVID-19 pandemic because lock-down forced customers to use self-servicing. After all, the traditional branches were not open. However, it is important to note that not all services can be covered by self-servicing and that some customers regardless will want to still speak to a human.
Evolution of products	The impact on this area is positive. While self-service is not primarily implemented for product improvement, it does have a positive side effect. Self-servicing allows firms to study customer behavior which means firms can either develop new products or enhance existing ones for the benefit of customers.
Lack of trust	The impact on this area is neutral. There is no real material impact in this area apart from self-servicing to improve customer satisfaction which should, in turn, improve trust in the financial services industry. However, it is important to note that not all services can be covered by self-servicing and that some customers regardless will want to still speak to a human. Therefore, these need to be catered for and if they are missed then it will reduce customer satisfaction which will increase the perception that financial services firms are only implementing self-servicing to benefit themselves.

(Continued)

Table 6.1 (Continued)

Accurate data	The impact on this area is negative. To allow self-servicing to work efficiently, the firms need to (a) have both clean and accurate client data and (b) have a client-centric view of clients and their products. Most firms struggle with this and will have to execute specific data cleansing projects to clean up their client data. However, even when this has been completed then new procedures and processes will need to implement to ensure the data stays clean.
Poor operating and technology models	The impact on this area is negative. Implementing self-service involves implementing another layer of complexity onto already complex and stretched operating models. Technology needs to be implemented to support the customer-facing applications, to ensure there is sufficient security in place, and to allow integrations with back-end systems.
Profitability/Cost drivers	The impact on these areas is positive. One of the key benefits of self-servicing is to reduce operating costs by removing the need for staff and buildings. However, it must be noted that there is a large up-front investment required to implement self-servicing which means the payback could be lengthy.
Changing nature of the workforce	The impact on this area is neutral. While there will be a reduction in the number of customer-facing staff because they will be replaced by the self-servicing platform, there will be opportunities for technology staff because skills will be required to implement and support the new self-servicing platform.
New competition and replacements	The impact on this area is positive at an industry level. Self-servicing has allowed new entrants to the market quickly and offers new, cheaper, and innovative products to customers. Although existing firms may not see this as a good thing because they could lose their market share.
Risk profile	The impact on this area is neutral. While implementing self-servicing has reduced risk because it ensures that activity is processed in the same controlled way, it has also increased risk because of the extra complexity with firms' operating models.

Case Study

The firm in question was an existing investment manager who was slow on implementing a self-servicing platform. While they were not losing existing customers, they were struggling to obtain new customers.

Their first immediate problem was the firm had client data spread across multiple product-based systems and this data was inconsistent with different naming conventions, addresses being recorded differently, and a large amount of missing data (such as postcodes and zip codes).

Therefore, to cleanse this data then all client data was sent to an external data cleansing firm who reviewed all the data, standardized it, and filled in any missing gaps. The process was very challenging and involved several cycles of cleaning and reviewing. The data cleansing firm was also able to access the same client across the different product systems using the client name, postcode, tax identifier, and date-of-birth as links. Once this was completed then the cleaned data was loaded back into the product-based systems and strict business controls were implemented to ensure the data quality was maintained. Also, the single list of client data was used to create a client-centric view of products, and interfaces were implemented to ensure any amendments made in the product systems were passed into this view.

This "clean data" provided a solid base to build their self-servicing offering upon.

However, the firm did not have any self-servicing technology which mean it was required a big, costly, and risky implementation. Therefore, the firm decided to build the platform but in a gradual manner. This would allow it to be launched quicker, allow the support team to be grown gradually and allow the firm to learn from its mistakes as future functionality was being released. Consequently, the core infrastructure was developed which integrated all the required back-end systems to the self-servicing platform. A customer application and website were developed but it only had one piece of function which was to open an account. This was launched and its usage was monitored.

As the firm became more confident, they started to roll out new functionality (such as balances, transaction reporting, and maintaining client details).

Summary

It is safe to say that the use of self-serving is a growing trend within Financial Services. It offers customers benefits (through better functionality, quicker access to their data, and wider access window). As noted earlier in this chapter, Deloitte's "Realizing the digital promise" report published in 2020 stated that 35 percent of various banks' customers increased their use of online banking during the pandemic. This trend is expected to continue.

It also offers benefits to firms by keeping their costs down, offering better services to clients, and allowing firms to understand customer behaviors which will help improve customer services and new product offerings.

However, some issues need to be understood. When firms start to implement self-servicing platforms, they need to ensure they have a clear reason for implementation (which is linked to the firms' overall strategy). Also, firms need to understand that the change will impact all areas of the firm. Operating models will become more complex as new technology to support self-servicing is "bolted" on. Complex security capabilities need to be implemented to ensure firms and customers are protected. Firms need to ensure they have accurate client data to support their self-servicing platforms. There will also be changes to the workforce as customer staff are not needed although additional technology staff will be required to support the new technology required.

While there is no clear movement, it is expected that the regulators will start to take an interest in self-servicing, especially as it becomes more popular. Their interest is likely to be around ensuring it benefits the customer, works as planned, and is resilient.

A final impact is that self-service has allowed new entrants to enter the market reasonably quickly. This has allowed new, cheaper, and innovative products to be launched. This will benefit customers although it could mean existing firms losing market share.

CHAPTER 7

Trend 3—Machine Learning

Introduction

What Is Machine Learning?

Machine Learning (ML) is a discipline within artificial intelligence (AI) that allows computer systems to learn and improve automatically without being specifically programmed. ML will take structured (such as database records) and unstructured data (such as images and voice recordings) and then analyze it to look for hidden patterns, dependencies, and so on which can then be used to develop predictive or explanatory models. These models can then be used for future decision making. For example, historic traffic records can be assessed to develop models that can be used to manage future traffic flows more effectively.

The growth of ML has been supported by several complementary technologies such as larger data sets (see Chapter 13 on Big Data and Chapter 10 on Natural Language Processing (NLP)), more and cheaper processing power (see Chapter 12 on Cloud Computing), and the development of programming languages that help computers "learn."

ML provides several key benefits:

1. The models developed are capable of learning and updating themselves as new and more data is received. Therefore a team of programmers is not required.
2. Once developed the models can be re-run as many times as possible to assess different situations.
3. The models can see patterns, trends, correlations, and so on that a human may not see quickly or even at all.
4. Finally, the models can be used on a wide range of applications. For example, weather prediction, health management, financial services, and so on.

How Does ML Work?

As mentioned above, ML builds a model based on historic data but how does this work?

To develop an ML model, a set of data is required that covers the situation that needs to be assessed. For example, if a firm is looking to test trading patterns then a large amount of trading data is required. This means that the model development is very reliant on the data being used to develop it. Therefore, if the data is poor, has gaps, is wrong, and so on then, it will cause problems with the model development.

When the data set has been obtained, it needs to be split randomly into two sets. The first set is the training set which will be used to "train" (or build or develop) the model and the second set is called the testing set which is used to test the model created. There are no clear rules on the split between the data sets but typically 70 percent of the data is used for "training" with 30 percent used for testing.

Once the data sets are split then the model can be developed. There are four main methods:

Supervised Learning

This method uses labeled data to determine the relationship between several input variables (called independent variables) and a known output (called dependent variables) to try and explain an existing outcome. For example, if one is assessing what makes certain trading profitable, the input/independent variables could be asset class, price, time of day, venue, trader, and so on and the output/dependent variable would be how profitable (or not) the trade is. Therefore, the key point is understanding both the relationship and the strength of this relationship between the independent variable(s) and subsequently dependent variable(s).

There are various ways in which supervised models could be developed:

1. Regression Analysis—This is to investigate where one variable impacts another. For example, the earlier in the day that a trade is executed then the more likely it is going to be profitable.
2. Decision Trees—This is a decision support process that uses a hierarchical or tree-like structure to allow decisions to be made.

3. Neural Networks—This is a model that is based on the human brain and nervous system. It allows levels of analysis between input and output variables. Typically these are developed by computer systems because of their complexity. However, this means that they can be hard to understand and follow by humans.

Unsupervised Learning

This uses unlabeled data where the input/independent and output/ dependent variables are not known at the start. As opposed to looking for relationships (like Supervised Learning), this model development process looks at hidden patterns or themes that were not immediately obvious. This is advantageous because it will help discover unknowns or things that one may have not even considered. For example, what types of customers buy certain products, how do people use a firm's website, and so on? However, it could also produce some useless patterns. Therefore, it is important to question any outputs and not to blindly follow everything that has been developed.

There are several model techniques but the most common is cluster analysis where data is grouped around similar properties. For example, trades done between 9 a.m. and 9.30 a.m. are typically profitable but trades done after 3 p.m. are normally unprofitable.

Semi-Supervised Learning

As the name implies, this is a halfway house between supervised and unsupervised learning. During the training stage, it uses a smaller labeled data set to help with classification and to help extraction from a larger unlabeled data set. This can help with solving the problem of not having sufficient data labeled data to train using a supervised learning approach.

Re-Enforced

This is a more complex and advanced technique than the above three. This approach is a cyclical approach where a model is initially built and then tested through trial and error until the model is as good as it can be. For example, a model could be developed around trading which is initially developed and tested for some cycles against real trader activity, and once the firm is happy then the model can be used for in "real world."

Uses With Financial Services

The use of ML within Financial Services is growing and all firms are either investigating or using it in some form or another.

Fraud and Anti-Money Laundering (AML)

One of the most common uses of ML is fraud and AML detection across all areas of a firm's business. One example is during the client take-on process where models can be developed to assess the risks of the potential new client which will allow a firm to determine whether the client can be onboarded and, if so, should any specific monitoring be implemented. A second example is to assess for internal fraud. Trading activity, communications, and other activities can be processed through models to assess whether any behavior is a symptom of fraud.

Insurance Checks

Insurance firms are using ML developed models to assess insurance premiums and the associated risk exposure, underwriting exposures, and pricing models. New insurance applications can be assessed to determine the risks which will allow firms to set an acceptable premium or even reject the business. Likewise, existing premiums can be assessed at renewal dates based in light of new risks gained and market movements which will allow the firm to either terminate the insurance on renewal, re-insurance parts, or all of the exposure or increase premiums.

Trading

ML models are being used in many methods. One example is that models have been developed to assess the risk exposure on stock portfolios around market changes and/or political events. In the event of possible issues, preventative action (say around executing buys/sells or amending hedging positions) can be performed. Likewise, traders have developed algorithmic trading models where ML can be used to assess previous trading patterns to ensure that future trading is more profitable or efficient.

Understand Customer Behavior

ML has been used to assess client historic behavior to predict future customer behavior. This has allowed customer-servicing improvements to be made around the types of customers and their requests when they happen and so on.

Improve Operating Efficiency

Firms have used ML techniques to model and understand their own internal operating efficiencies. For example, understanding which processes work well, which processes have blockages, which processes are manually intensive, and so on. This has allowed improvements to be made such as implementing new technology such as Robotic Processing Automation (see Chapter 8).

Cross and Increased Selling of Financial Products

One of the key benefits of ML is that it has allowed customer behaviors to be modeled, understood, and predicted. Apart from understanding customer behavior and improving customer servicing (see above), it has allowed firms to historically understand which products customers prefer so that these can be cross-sold to existing or new customers in the future.

Firms Are Starting to Increasingly Use ML

According to a 2021 report published by the London Stock Exchange Group called "The defining moment for data scientists", of 482 firms surveyed (covering 165 Asia Pacific, 162 EMEA, and 155 North America) 80 percent are now using ML as part of their operations with 46 percent using ML for core business functions (such as those listed under those listed earlier on this page as well as page 84 above).

Challenges of ML

Even though ML gives firms several great benefits, it is a challenging technology to implement and requires a large amount of thought and focus.

What Is the Business Reason to Implement ML?

There are many stories of firms (not just in Financial Services) implementing new technology for the sake of the technology as opposed to implementing technology to meet some type of business or strategic need. In the same way as any major change, this means before embarking on an ML implementation, a firm must have a clear business reason to implement the technology. Please refer to Appendix B for a list of the variables to be discussed when completing a Business Case.

Start Small and Then Grow Implementation

There is a clear tendency to try and implement new technology too quickly. This is because people get "carried away with the technology." This is especially true in Financial Services. However, implementing any new technology is a challenging process and it should be taken gradually with regular point reviews.

Therefore, it is normally advisable to perform some sort of pilot implementation to assess whether the technology works? Does it offer the benefits promised? And does the firm have the skills to implement the technology? The results of the pilot study can inform the rest of the implementation. For example, how quickly should the roll-out be performed? What skills are needed? Will ML provide the benefits promised? and so on. It is not that uncommon for firms to considerably rethink ML projects after the pilot stage because the technology is more complex or costly than originally thought.

Even once the pilot study is completed then a gradual rollout plan should be implemented. This allows the firm to understand the technology and associated impacts as well as build confidence, momentum, and a return on investment with senior management.

Beware of Handing Over Full Control to the Computer

People are generally nervous about handing over full control to a computer system. There are various Hollywood blockbusters where technology has been handed over to a computer that has gone rogue and taken over the world.

While this is unlikely to happen with ML in Financial Services, some sort of caution is needed.

ML models are developed by computers which means they can be challenging to fully understand. Some computer-generated Neural Networks are almost impossible to fully understand unless one spends days and days working through them. Also, some of the models may produce odd results. While this could be correct, this could also be wrong. For example, imagine the issues and problems if automated trading or fraud detection models were not working fully.

Therefore, for critical processes (say fraud assessments), a human check needs to be in the process to ensure what the model is suggested sounds credible. Also for fully automated processes (e.g., trading activity), there needs to be some sort of "circuit breaker" to stop the model if it appears to be going "astray."

Remember That ML Models Have Been Developed/Tested Using Historic Data

One key point to note is that while ML models are used to predict future behaviors, they are developed and tested using historic data.

Therefore, there is a real risk that once a model is developed and running live then new data and situations will be generated which means the model is at best out-of-date or stale and at worse producing misleading or dangerous predictions.

This can be mitigated in two ways. One method is to have more than one model to predict a situation. The outputs of these models can be compared to see if any differences could be caused by the model becoming stale. The second model is to constantly update and back-test the model as new data becomes available. This will ensure the model is constantly kept up-to-date.

The Importance of Good, Timely, and Accurate Data

As stated previously, ML models are built on data and use data for their predictions. This means they are massively reliant on timely and accurate data. If there are problems with the data (say it is wrong, there are gaps, etc.), it could be that the model is developed wrong and the predictions it generates are also wrong.

Therefore, firms need to ensure that all data required is timely and accurate.

Unfortunately, problems are only uncovered once they happen, so one method to mitigate against poor data is to have more than one model to predict a situation. The outputs of these models can be compared to see if any differences could be caused by poor data.

Make Sure the Model (or Models) Works

While the points above have focused on the importance of data being correct and complete, it is also important to ensure that the developed models work as hoped for.

Firstly is the correct model development technique being used? For example for supervised learning are the correct independent variables informing the required dependent variables, or for unsupervised learning then do the patterns generated look realistic? Therefore, for this reason, it is recommended that multiple different models are developed using different development techniques. This will provide several models whose outputs can be compared to help highlight any issues.

Secondly, the models will need to be carefully tested. This can be a time-consuming process, especially if more than one model needs to be tested. However one of the key questions to ask when testing is "does the outputs of the model make sense?" As ML models are developed using computers on a data set, some strange results are possible especially if the data has gaps or errors within it. Therefore, if the outputs or themes appear "odd" then do not be afraid to revisit the models.

A New Firm Capability Will Be Required to Support ML

Implementing ML requires firms to build a new capability. This covers new technology people with the appropriate skills and processes to control them both.

The new technology requires the following components:

- Suitable data will be required for both the development/ testing of the models as well as the normal day-to-day running. This timely and accurate data may need to be obtained from various sources, cleansed, and loaded for processing. This area has been helped by the development of Big Data technologies (see Chapter 13).
- Once the data is available then it may require considerable processing power to both build/test and run the models on a day-to-day basis. This can be housed on in-house services but this can be complex and costly. Therefore, firms are looking to use Cloud computing technologies for this (see Chapter 12).
- A platform will also be needed to host the development/ testing and running of the ML models. These are specific platforms developed specifically for this purpose. While there are many platforms available they are complex and need specially trained staff to operate. Also, the firm will need to ensure they select the relevant supplier around functionality fit, cost fit, commercial fit, and cultural fit because once the platform (and supplier) is selected then the firm will need to work with them for a long period.

These new technologies may need to be procured from a vendor or supplier. Because of the cost, importance, and complexity of ML then an appropriate supplier must be selected. Therefore, please see Appendix A which guides on selecting a supplier.

Suitably skilled people will need to be recruited to develop/test the models initially as well as support them on an ongoing basis. Three types of skillset are required: (a) people who understand ML techniques at a conceptual level, (b) people who understand financial services, and

(c) people who understand the technologies and ML platforms selected. Typically, firms will recruit expert consultants initially because it is quicker although these consultants can be expensive and there is a risk of relying on external consultants. Therefore as part of the project, firms will need to either train existing internal staff and/or recruit permanent staff as required.

Finally, processes and controls will be around which activities should be using ML, how models are developed/tested, how models are rolled out, how their usage is tracked, and how models are reviewed regularly.

Ensure There Is Sufficient Governance and Control in Place

While ML offers good opportunities it does create several risks that need to be governed and controlled. ML models can be complex or sometimes impossible to fully understand which is a danger as firms become more and more reliant on them. Therefore, firms need to implement policies, controls, and oversight around which activities should be using ML, how models are developed/tested, how models are rolled out, how their usage is tracked, and how models are reviewed regularly. Any problems found should be escalated to senior management in the same way as any other risk or issue.

Customers or Staff Do Not Like Being Monitored

While ML will allow customer behavior to be understood which will allow improvements in customer servicing and products to be made, customers can be nervous, or skeptical about being monitored. In the same way, firms are using ML to monitor staff behavior around improving operational efficiency and fraud detection.

In effect, they may see firms as a "big brother" overlooking them.

Therefore, firms need to be open about what they are using ML for anyhow it will benefit the customer and their staff.

Future Challenges

Table 7.1 Future Challenges for Machine Learning

Area	Details
Increased regulations	The regulatory impact is still unclear in this area. While ML has data analysis at its center then firms are subject to various data protection legislation in place. For example, GDPR in the EU and UK. However, it is reasonable to suspect that if ML and its usage increase as predicted then regulators will look to rules to regulate its implementation and usage.
Changing nature of clients	ML should provide advantages to customers. Firms are using ML to understand customer behavior which should allow improvements in customer servicing to be made and allow better and more appropriate products to be developed to help customers. Firms are also using ML to obtain operating efficiencies and any associated cost savings should be able to be passed onto customers as lower fees.
Evolution of products	ML should help firms develop better products. Firms are using ML to understand customer behavior which should allow better and more appropriate products to be developed to help customers.
Lack of trust	The impact in this area is neutral at the moment. While ML will allow customer behavior to be understood which will allow improvements in customer servicing and products to be made, customers can be nervous or skeptical about being monitored. In effect, they may see firms as a "big brother" overlooking them. Therefore, firms need to be open about what they are using ML for and how it will benefit the customer.
Accurate data	This impact is impacted adversely. The development, testing, and running of ML models are very reliant on timely, accurate, and complete data. If the data has issues then the models will not work. Therefore, firms will need to implement technology, process, controls, and oversight to ensure all data used is as correct as possible with any issues being identified.

(Continued)

Table 7.1 (Continued)

Poor operating and technology models	This impact is impacted adversely. ML is another operating model or technology component that will need to be "plugged" into a firms' existing complex operating models. This extra component will need to be supported by suitably skilled people, processes, and systems in conjunction with possible external suppliers. The result is that firms' operating model's complexity, cost, and risk profile increase.
Profitability/Cost Drivers	ML should in the long term (at least) support firms in improving their profitability. Modeling customer behavior should allow better products, cross-selling, and improved customer servicing. This should stop customers from leaving as well as attract new customers. The result should be an increase in revenue. Likewise using ML to reduce risk events (such as fraud) and improve operational efficiency should reduce operating costs. However, it is important to note that ML will require a cost to implement as well as additional running costs. Therefore (as part of the business case), firms need to understand any payback period.
Changing nature of the workforce	The impact on this area is generally positive. ML requires new skills. This covers both understanding ML at a conceptual level and also understanding the technologies to develop and build models. This offers career development possibilities for staff. However, there is one possible downside. As ML models are being used to improve operating model efficiency then there is a possibility that some staff could either lose or have their jobs change as a result.
New competition and replacements	The impact on this area is positive to the customer. This is because new and/or more agile firms may be able to ML to develop more innovative, functionality-rich, and better products for customers. This is good news for customers but a risk for other firms.
Risk profile	The impact on this area is neutral. ML does create risks about another piece of technology that needs to be supported by an existing complex operating model. Also as vendor platforms are often used then the risk of supplier reliance increases as well. But if it is implemented fully then it will reduce risks around fraud, operating inefficiencies, poor customer service, and losing revenue.

Case Study

A firm was concerned that certain members of its staff were committing fraud or just behaving irresponsibly. Therefore, they decided to develop a model (based on ML techniques) to try and assess the situation.

Data was gathered across fraudulent occurrences, trading activities, chat, e-mail, telephones, and instant messaging. This data was used to develop and test a set of ML-based models using unsupervised learning to determine what patterns of behavior are likely to have caused fraudulent behavior.

Once the model was developed and tested, it was run on a regular weekly basis where data was gathered, run through it and any possible fraudulent activity was identified. Each possible occurrence was then investigated by the internal (human) fraud team to see if it was a real issue or just a "false negative." If after investigation it was a fraud then it was progressed through the relevant procedures. If after investigation it was not fraud then the reason for its appearance was investigated and if necessary the model was enhanced to try and stop it from appearing again.

Summary

ML is an emerging technology that is being increasingly used with Financial Services (in such areas as fraud detection, insurance risk management, trading, understanding customer behavior, and implementing operational efficiencies). As discussed above, according to a 2021 report published by the London Stock Exchange Group called "The defining moment for data scientists", of 482 firms surveyed (split 165 Asia Pacific, 162 EMEA, and 155 North America) 80 percent are now using ML as part of the normal operations with 46 percent using ML for core business functions.

However, like all emerging technologies, there are a few points of caution to note:

- It is a large and costly implementation. Therefore, firms need a clear upfront reason to implement (with a supporting business case) that is linked to the organization's strategy. Firms should understand implementation/ongoing costs and risks. The implementation itself should be a gradual rollout to ensure the firms understand the changes and to determine whether the benefits are genuine.

- ML is very reliant on timely and accurate data. If the firm cannot obtain suitably accurate and timely data then the implementation will struggle to succeed. Firms need to also understand that once the models are developed and running then the data that informs them will need to be reviewed to (a) ensure any changes in the data are highlighted and if required (b) the models are updated. Firms also need to be aware that if events happen have not been seen before then any ML rules developed and tested could produce some unexpected actions.

- Firms will need to create new capabilities to implement and support ML. New technology will need to be deployed and integrated with firms existing complex and strained operating models. This technology will need to be provided by a supplier so this creates supplier reliance risk. Staff will be needed with suitable skills around understanding ML techniques, the financial services industry, and the ML platform selected. This may require recruiting consultants initially but then training existing staff and recruiting new permanent employees later. Finally, new processes, policies, and controls will be required around the usage, testing, and deployment of ML models.

- Finally, some ethical issues need addressing. While ML is normally implemented for the best of reasons, customers and staff will feel uncomfortable if they feel their actions are being monitored. Therefore, firms need to be clear and upfront about their usages.

CHAPTER 8

Trend 4—Robotic Process Automation (RPA)

Introduction

What Is Robotic Process Automation?

Robotic Process Automation (RPA) is using a robotic software programme (or bots) to imitate the processing that a human person would do on their desktop. In effect, the bot is replacing the human person.

How Does RPA Work?

RPA bots are developed by typically a third party RPA platform recording the actions that an end-user would normally follow to complete a process. This would cover recording clicks, drop-down selections, entering text, pressing return, opening folders, copying files, and so on. Once the recordings are made then they can be tested to ensure they cover all scenarios and perfected as required. Once they are working they can be promoted into the production environment for live running.

RPA works best on a business process that is simple, rule-based, uses structured data, and does not change regularly. For example, a bot could be developed to automatically forward e-mails onto a pre-defined distribution list or to automatically copy data from a spreadsheet into a separate file which is then copied into another folder. RPA does struggle with processes that are complex to define (such as processing the death of a customer), processes that have a complex set of steps (such as dealing with customer complaints), or processes that do not have a pre-defined set of rules.

In effect, RPA allows a workflow to be implemented quicker and cheaper. Workflow systems are complex, costly, and take a long time to be fully implemented. They also often require changes to applications or APIs (Application Programme Interfaces) to be built to allow the workflow system to obtain the data it needs.

There are many general key benefits for RPA:

- RPA bots are built on top of the existing operating model and will also mirror the current processes. Therefore, automation can be implemented reasonably quickly and cheaply without the need to enhance technology systems by developing APIs and other major changes.
- RPA bots allow the operating model to be streamlined and made efficient. It allows staff levels to be reduced as bots replace the work they do. These staff can either be lost (and therefore resulting in cost savings) or be redeployed doing other more high-level tasks (such as customer servicing).
- RPA bots can run full time—that is 24 hours per day across 365 days per year. This gives more processing capacity. Staff are unable to work for these long periods.
- Assuming (a) the bots are developed and tested fully and (b) the processes or environment does not change then the error rates will be reduced or even cut to zero. The rules developed will be following consistency at all times. Humans are susceptible to errors and mistakes.
- RPA is good for simple and repetitive tasks (such as copying files) which humans may find boring and laborious to perform. This boredom will mean the human is not 100 percent focused on the task which will result in errors and mistakes.
- RPA allows simpler and easier scalability. If processing volumes need to increase then extra bots and/or processing power can be added quickly and relatively cheaply. Likewise, if processing volumes decrease then bots can be removed just as quickly. If these processes were run by a human team then scaling up would involve a lengthy and possibly costly

recruitment process followed by several weeks of on-the-job training, and any scaling down could result in staff redundancies and/or redeployments.

- While there is an implementation cost (see below) that could take a while to pay back, RPA tends to be cheaper to operate on a day-to-day basis than having a team of humans running the processes.
- By moving the simple and easily codified processes on RPA then it allows firms to release staff to work on "value-added" tasks such as dealing with customer queries, cross-selling, and so on.
- Using RPA provides Business Continuity Processing (BCP) improvements around reducing complexity and cost. If there is a large human team then it will require spare desks, buildings, possible remote connections, and so on to ensure sufficient BCP is in place. If processes are running on RPA then as long as the infrastructure running then is resilient then there is no need for desks, people, remote connections, and so on.

Uses of RPA Within the Financial Services Industry

In effect, any process that can be easily codified can be supported by RPA. Therefore, firms are using RPA in several different areas. For example:

- Bank Reconciliations—A bot is developed to download the required data from the banking system and internal financial systems. This data is then automatically compared (say) using a spreadsheet with any exceptions being highlighted and e-mailed to relevant staff for investigation.
- Client Servicing—A bot can be written that will receive in e-mails and then review the title and/or look for keywords in the body of the e-mail. Depending on a set of rules the e-mail can be forwarded to the relevant team(s) that need to investigate the client request.
- Downloading and directing of data—Bots can be developed that will download data (say market index or prices data),

reformat it using a series of spreadsheets, and then copy or
e-mail this data into a pre-defined list of recipients.

- Some firms have used bots to perform overnight processing.
This could cover triggering certain jobs and then waiting until
they are completed, and e-mailing interested people to let
them know.

- Also, some firms have used RPA to help automate testing
software changes. Bots are developed to replicate standard
business processes such as creating clients, amending clients,
processing a bank transfer, producing a statement, and so on,
and then they are used to create test data, perform tests, and
so on. Once the bots are developed then they can be used
time after time thus making testing a quicker process.

- Account Opening—This is an essential process but manual
and laborious to complete. Therefore, bots have been developed which will receive in a structured request to open an
account from a prospect. This request is normally from a
mobile/tablet app, website, or structured e-mail. The bot will
review the application for completeness, perform all required
checks (such as KYC, criminal, or fraud checks), request
any further information needed and, once everything is in
order, then formally open the account and issue any required
documentation to the client. If issues are encountered then
the request will be rejected and passed to a human team to
investigate.

- Accounting Closing—Similar to the Account Opening above,
this is another essential but manual process. Therefore bots
have been developed to receive a structured request to close
an account. (This request is normally from a mobile/tablet
app, website, or a structured e-mail). The bot will perform all
required checks and request any missing information. Once
everything is satisfactory then the bot will close the account
and issue any closing documents. If problems are encountered
then the request will be rejected and passed to a human team
to investigate.

- Blocking stolen or lost credit, debit and/or payment cards— Once a client discovers that their card is missing or lost then they will start to panic and will demand the card be blocked immediately. Therefore, bots have been developed which will make this process much quicker and more efficient. The bot will receive a structured notification that a credit, debit, or payment card is either lost or stolen. Per the earlier examples, this request is normally from a mobile/tablet app, website, or structured e-mail. The bot will perform any necessary checks to confirm the request is genuine, and if everything is valid then the offending card will be blocked or stopped and the client notified. If difficulties are encountered then the request will be rejected and passed to a human team to investigate.

- Processing trades and/or transfers—Firms have developed bots to help automate trading and transfers. The bot will receive a structured request (from a mobile/tablet app, website, or a structured e-mail) to either process a trade or perform a transfer. The bot will validate the request and if everything is correct, the requested trade or transfer will be executed. If problems are encountered then the request will be rejected and handed to a human team to investigate.

- Providing pre-sales documentation—Firms are requested by prospects to provide brochures and marketing information to prospects. This is an essential process but it is manually inten- sive and laborious. Therefore, firms have developed bots that will receive in the literature request (from a mobile/tablet app, website, or a structured e-mail), determine what documents are required, send them to the prospect, and then record the request on a sales system so the prospect can be tracked if required.

- Fulfill client documentation requests—Nowadays firms receive a large number of requests for documentation to meet the needs of the auditors, the police, the tax authorities, sub- poenas plus many others. These requests normally need to be completed within a matter of days but obtaining the required documents is a complex and laborious process because the required documents are often stored across a variety of folders, application systems, and document repositories. However, firms have developed bots that will receive in the client reference then automatically scan or search all the required folders, software applications, and repositories for documents with minimal manual impact. Once the documents have been found then they can be issued as required.

Challenges of RPA

Do Not Underestimate the Size of the Change Required to Implement RPA Successfully

While developing, testing, and implementing RPA bots sounds simple and RPA is often mentioned as a quick way to implement workflow, it is still a challenging implementation. It should be viewed similar to any major technology implementation and not just something that can be done "part-time." It impacts all areas of people, organizational structure, processes, technology, and so on. It is not just a technology rollout. Therefore, firms need to be aware that it will take time, there will be problems and firms need to be prepared for the "long run."

It will involve a large amount of support from all levels of the firms. This covers senior management down to the most junior members of staff.

Have a Clear Business Reason to Implement RPA with Clearly Defined Success Criteria

There are many stories of firms (not just in the Financial Services) implementing new technology for the sake of the technology as opposed to implementing technology to meet some type of business or strategic need. (In the same way as any major change) this means before embarking on an RPA implementation then a firm must have a clear business reason to implement the technology. Please refer to Appendix B for a list of the variables to be discussed when completing a Business Case.

Implement or Roll Out RPA in a Slow Phased Approach

As mentioned earlier an implementation plan needs to be created to implement the RPA platform with the associate bots and integrations.

It is important to remember that RPA is a large implementation which means it can be risky. Therefore, it would be sensible to structure the plan around a phased approach. The initial phase would contain the implementation of the actual core platform but then there should be phases each containing a prioritized set of processes or bots. The prioritization should focus on the processes that are (a) easier to define and therefore code as a bot and (b) the processes that offer the most business benefit. This approach will hopefully ensure the project delivers some immediate benefits which will create goodwill, momentum, and confidence. It will also help with financial payback and allow the firm to learn about RPA which could provide useful lessons for the future.

It is also important to understand what is needed to support the implementation. This could involve staffing such as senior management, operational staff, in-house technology staff, RPA platform vendor staff, technology staff who support the systems being integrated with, legal staff, and compliance staff plus others. Furthermore, if the rollout of RPA involves staff losing their jobs then (a) these staff may need to be involved in the project which (b) will require careful and tactful management.

Finally, it may also be necessary to ensure there is desk space for the team, test environments, shared document folders, e-mail lists, and so on.

Build an RPA Capability Covering Technology, Processes, and People

The actual platform consists of three parts: (a) the technology platform, (b) the new processes and oversight required to monitor RPA, and (c) the new skills that are required to run RPA.

Technology Platform

This is a key decision because if the wrong or inappropriate technology platform is selected then it will cause issues during implementation and day-to-day basis, which will ultimately cause the change to fail.

It is possible to develop an in-house technology platform to develop and run the RPA bots but this could be complex and costly. There are a variety of third packages that could be used and it would seem sensible to use one of these. These platforms range from very functionality-rich (and costly) platforms that offer a wide range of features to simpler platforms that do not offer a massive range of features but are often much cheaper and less complex to operate.

Therefore, some types of formal technology platform vendor selection process must be followed. Please see Appendix A which contains a list of the checks to be performed when selecting a supplier.

New Governance and Oversight Processes

As well as the implementation of the technology, new processes, and governance frameworks will need to be designed and implemented to control the new technology. This will cover four main areas:

- Oversight of the daily processes—Controls need to be in place to ensure the bots work as designed. Any issues or problems need to be identified and trapped immediately. Once identified then the cause needs to be investigated so both (a) any historic activity can be fixed and (b) the bot can be fixed to stop the problem from happening in the future. Any material issues will need escalating to management.
- Oversight of the supplier—The firm will likely be reliant on the supplier in some way. This could cover areas such as hosting the platform, supporting the bots, providing support, providing consultancy, and so on. Therefore, controls and oversight need to be in place to allow the firm to monitor the supplier to ensure they do what they have committed to in the contract. For example, are support calls being responded to per schedule? Are there issues with the hosting? and so on. If there are issues then these need to be escalated to senior management at both the supplier and firm.

- Change control process—Bots will need to be added, updated, or removed. This could cover activity as part of the implementation project or part of business-as-usual running. Therefore, there needs to be a process to ensure changes are made safely to ensure existing bots are not impacted adversely. Depending on the involvement of the supplier (such as hosting the platform) then they may need to be involved as part of this process.
- Policies for the development of bots—Good standards need to be created around the development of bots. This will cover programming standards, integration standards, information security standards, testing standards, version control, and release procedures. Depending on the involvement of the supplier then the supplier may need to be involved as part of this process.

Ensuring the Firm Has Sufficiently Skilled Staff to Support RPA Once the Project Completes

A dedicated project team will have been formed to implement the initial RPA project. This will have consisted of senior management to provide oversight and steer plus many "on the ground" people who would perform the developments, integrations, and so on required. This group of people would have been sourced from in-house staff, contractors, consultants, and possibly staff from the platform vendor.

Therefore, firms must develop the necessary skills to be able to support the RPA platform once the project closes, because otherwise they will be reliant on external contractors and platform vendor staff. This means that senior management will need to be educated on understanding RPA and its benefits at a general level. Also, more junior staff will need to be trained on RPA, the specific platform selected, the integration with back-end systems as well as the suite of bots developed and rolled out as part of the project. This training can be done by training existing staff but it may also be necessary to recruit new permanent staff with the required skillsets.

Future Challenges

Table 8.1 Future challenges of robotic process automation

Area	Details
Increased regulations	There are no specific regulations regarding RPA at the moment. Although the implementation of RPA could be covered by the various Operational Resilience regulation in progress. This regulation ensures firms have a mature and robust operating model supported by clear controls, decision-making processes, risk/issue management, BCP, senior management oversight, and management of suppliers. However, if RPA becomes more mainstream (or there are any major issues with RPA) then the regular will no doubt start to look at implementing regulation.
Changing nature of clients	RPA should have a positive impact on clients. As one of the key reasons for implementation is reducing risk, reducing costs, and improving efficiency then this should benefit clients in terms of better servicing and reduced fees.
Evolution of products	RPA should have a positive impact on clients. As one of the key reasons for implementation is reducing risk, reducing costs, and improving efficiency then this should benefit products in terms of making them easier to operate, allowing more complex features, and reducing running costs.
Lack of trust	The impact on this area is neutral. The only side effect could be that customers and the general public could be concerned about the robotic nature of RPA and think firms are losing control of their operating models. This could cause some unpopular media attention which will need to be managed.
Accurate data	This area is impacted negatively. For RPA and bots to work accurately (or even at all) then it needs clean, timely, and accurate data. Therefore, this puts more pressure on firms to ensure their data quality is good.
Poor operating and technology models	This area is impacted negatively. While RPA should help with codifying standard tasks and improving efficiency in general, it does involve adding another complex and business-critical component to firms' already existing stretching and complex operating models which increases the risk of issues and problems.

Profitability/cost drivers	RPA should have a positive impact from a long-term point of view. While there is no doubt a large cost to implement RPA, it will provide long-term financial benefits in terms of reduced staff, possible less office space, scalability, and control.
Changing nature of the workforce	The impact on this area is neutral. While some staff will lose their jobs (or have to change jobs) as a result of RPA, there is an opportunity for staff to develop new skills around implementing and supporting RPA.
New competition and replacements	The impact on this area is neutral. A new entrant may be able to use RPA to help with their operating model but they will still need to implement back-end systems, websites, and so on.
Risk profile	The impact on this area is neutral. While the implementation of RPA increases the risk and complexity of the operating model, it will allow processes to be standardized, monitored, and also be scalable which reduces the risk profile.

Case Study

A firm used RPA to improve its Know Your Customer checks.

Originally, the process was very heavily based on slow manual processes. The customer would send in their application electronically and the firm then had to cut-and-paste data from the application form into a web portal (owned by the KYC provider) who would then process the application and then e-mail back their response. These responses would be manually collated and reviewed by the business teams.

RPA was used to automate the process. The customer will still send in the electronic application form but it would be sent to a specific e-mail address where a bot would capture it, extract the required data, and automatically populate the KYC provider's web portal. When the KYC portal has a response then it would be e-mailed to another specific e-mail address where another bot would capture it, collate the responses, and send them automatically to the business teams for processing.

The implementation of RPA made a "clumsy" process much more robust, quicker, cost-effective, and scalable.

Summary

RPA is a very helpful emerging technology that allows firms to implement workflow (with the associated efficiency/control improvements and cost savings) without having to implement full workflow systems and the associated technology rewrites. It also provides benefits to customers and supports the products that firms offer.

However, it is important that while RPA is similar to implementing an enterprise workflow system, it is still a complex implementation and should be treated with the same amount of respect. If RPA is implemented poorly then it will cause problems with processes which (apart from increasing the complexity of the operating model) could cause material errors. Also to allow the cost savings to be made then firms may need to make staff redundant which will require careful and tactful management.

Therefore, firms need to have a clear business reason supported by a clear set of success criteria and a business case to support the implementation. While RPA provides costs savings in the long term, there will be a large up-front spend and implementation effort to implement the platform.

RPA only really works well on processes that can be defined easily and codified. Processes that cannot be codified easily (such as dealing with complex client questions) are not suitable for RPA.

RPA is also reliant on clean, timely, and accurate data. If the data is poor then the processes will not operate as designed which will cause problems.

Firms need to clearly define the operating platform for RPA. Most platforms are provided by third parties. So the vendor has to be carefully selected to ensure it is a strategic vendor that the firm will be able to work with in the future. The hosting of the platform needs to be investigated because both in-house and external (including Cloud) hosting has its own set of advantages and disadvantages. An effort will also be required to integrate the RPA bots with any existing back-end systems to allow the processes to work.

In addition to the technical aspects, firms need to implement oversight over the daily usage of the platform, any suppliers involved, change control processes, and policies to manage the development of bots.

It is also good practice to roll out RPA bots in a phased prioritized approach with the processes that offer maximum benefit being first. This approach will hopefully ensure that the project delivers some immediate benefits which will create goodwill, momentum, confidence, and some initial project payback.

Finally, there are no specific regulations concerning RPA at the moment (apart from the general need for firms to ensure they have a robust operating model). However, if RPA becomes more mainstream (or there are some major issues with RPA) then the regular will no doubt start to look at implementing regulation.

CHAPTER 9

Trend 5—Internet of Things

Introduction

What Is the Internet of Things?

The Internet of Things ("IoT" or sometimes the Internet of Everything) is taking the evolution of the Internet to the next logical stage by allowing any physical object (or "thing") to be added to the Internet. This is in addition to the traditional devices such as PCs, tablets, printers, and phones. These new objects (or "things") could be anything from photocopiers, security sensors, wearables (such as watches), and televisions.

The Main Uses of IoT

At a general level, the IoT has three main high-level uses:

- Firstly, it allows some sort of activity to be monitored remotely (such as a person's health, a gauge on a machine, or a security alarm) with no human interaction. Then if a pre-defined level is breached, an action is automatically triggered (such as calling a doctor, switching off a machine, or calling the police).
- Secondly, it allows data gathering to be performed remotely and with no human interaction. For example, IoT sensors are often implemented to record traffic volumes over periods on certain roads. This data can then be used (using Machine Learning techniques (see Chapter 7)) to model driver behavior so that planners can look to divert traffic in different ways to reduce congestion or even look to develop new roads.

- Finally, IoT allows technology to be used easier and more efficiently by humans. For example, people can connect to the Internet to request music by just using a watch or speaking into a speaker as opposed to using a bulky laptop or tablet. Another example is the Smart Home where all parts of a house (heating, locks, lighting, etc.) can be remotely controlled by the homeowner using an application.

Benefits of IoT

There are a variety of benefits of IoT at a general level:

- There is improved automation with less reliance on humans and people. This means that there should be fewer errors.
- Operations efficiency is improved and it is also more cost-effective. Real-time monitoring (with rules and triggers) will ensure operations are run better. This also allows better controls, the collection of better data, and also the better use of assets (such as powering down hardware that is not being used).
- IoT allows real-time and accurate data to be collected. This will help with understanding customer behavior which will help firms improve their customer servicing, improve their product offering, allow firms to cross-sell to existing customers, improve efficiency, and reduce costs.

Uses With Financial Services

Compared to some of the other emerging technology trends in this book, the use of IoT within financial services is not as advanced but there are still a variety of very good uses for IoT within Financial Services which are described below.

Monitor Financial Services Assets

Firms have a large number of physical assets which are critical to their operation and need to be maintained and managed.

- Automated Teller Machines (ATM)—While the use of cash is reducing, people still do use a large amount of cash and most people obtain cash from ATMs. Banks have implemented IoT sensors to monitor the usage of ATMs. The feedback from these sensors will allow banks to initially determine when cash levels are running low so they can be filled up. They are also looking to monitor ATM usage, length of queues, how many people leave the queue because of the long wait, and so on. This will allow banks to forward plan whether they need to implement new ATMs or remove underused ones.
- Branches—Banks have used IoT technologies to monitor the number of people who use their branches. These sensors will record how many people enter the branch, how many people leave the branch because the queues are too long, how long the queues are, and so on. This allows banks to determine their servicing levels in terms of staff, self-serving pods, and opening hours.

Provide Remote and Real-Time Customer Services

Providing remote customer servicing over PCs, tablets, and phones have been standard for many years now but IoT allows similar servicing to be provided using virtually any object that can be connected to the Internet. This covers wearables (e.g., a watch), smart TVs plus many others. This ensures that the customers can receive the benefit of instant client servicing if needed.

Collect Data on Customer Behavior

IoT allows firms to collect data on customer behavior which can then be used to improve customer servicing, enhance products, and allow firms to cross-sell their products. For example, an application can be implemented on a wearable (such as a watch) that will track what the customer does, where they go, what they spend their money on, and other behaviors. This data can then be used to improve customer servicing, develop more appropriate products, and also allow firms to cross-sell new products to existing customers.

Fraud Protection

IoT also allows firms to implement better fraud detection controls. For example, if a customer changes their details or makes a payment then a confirmation can be sent to a wearable device to ask them to confirm that they have performed this activity. Likewise, banks can use IoT wearables to determine where the client is to ensure they are in the same place that a payment is being made. If there is some difference then a confirmation can be sent to the client for confirmation.

Shock Treatments

IoT is being used to track customer spending. If the client is nearing (or has even breached) their credit or overdraft limit, then a message can be sent to a wearable to warn the client of this so either they can stop spending or look to transfer money into the offending account.

General Health of Customers

Firms are also using IoT technologies to try and generally increase the health and well-being of their customers. One large UK health insurer is offering points (which can lead to prizes such as a spa break) if their customers walk so many steps a day, sleep for so many hours, drink so many glasses of water, and so on.

Challenges of IoT

While IoT does have several real benefits, it does also pose some real challenges that firms will need to tackle for a successful implementation.

Clear Business Focus

There are many stories of firms (not just in the Financial Services) implementing new technology for the sake of the technology as opposed to implementing technology to meet some type of business or strategic need. (In the same way as any major change) this means before embarking on an IoT implementation, a firm must have a clear business reason to implement the technology.

Please refer to Appendix B for a list of variables to be discussed when completing a Business Case.

Start Small and Then Grow Implementation

There is a clear tendency to try and implement new technology too quickly. This is because people get carried away with technology. This is especially true in Financial Services. However, implementing any new technology is a challenging process and it should be taken gradually with regular point reviews.

Therefore, it is normally advisable to perform some sort of pilot implementation to assess whether the technology work? Does it offer the benefits promised? And does the firm have the skills to implement the technology? The results of the pilot study can inform the rest of the implementation. For example, how quickly should the roll-out be performed? What skills are needed? Will IoT provide the benefits promised? And so on. It is not that uncommon for firms to considerably rethink IoT projects after the pilot stage because the technology is more complex or costly than originally thought.

Even once the pilot study is completed then a gradual rollout plan should be implemented. This allows the firm to understand the technology and associated impacts as well as build confidence, momentum, and a return on investment with senior management and if any major issues are encountered, it is easier to roll back a new facility from a small subset of "tame" customers (staff, partners, "friends and family," etc.) than from the entire customer base.

Build an IoT Capability Covering Technology, Processes, and People

The actual platform consists of three parts: (a) the technology platform, (b) the new processes and oversight required to monitor IoT, and (c) the new skills that are required to run IoT.

Technology Platform

This is a key decision because if the wrong or inappropriate technology platform is selected then it will cause issues during implementation and day-to-day basis, which will ultimately cause the change to fail.

It is possible to develop an in-house technology platform to develop and support IoT but this could be complex and costly. There are a variety of third-party packages that could be used and it would seem sensible to use one of these. These platforms range from very functionality-rich (and often costly) platforms that offer a wide range of features to simpler platforms that do not offer a massive range of features but are often much cheaper and less complex to implement and operate. Therefore, some type of formal technology platform vendor selection process must be followed. Please see Appendix A which contains a list of the checks to be performed when selecting a supplier.

Also, any new IoT infrastructure will need to be integrated with the existing backend systems used by the firms. These existing systems are likely to be legacy, supported by a combination of in-house and external suppliers, and use a range of different technologies. The result is that the operational model becomes increasingly more complex and risky to support.

New Governance and Oversight Processes

As well as the implementation of the technology, new processes, and governance frameworks will need to be designed and implemented to control the new technology. This will cover four main areas.

- Oversight of the daily processes—Controls need to be in place to ensure IoT works as designed. If problems are identified then the cause needs to be discovered so the problem can be addressed to stop the problem from happening in the future. Any material issues will need escalating to management.
- Oversight of the supplier—The firm will likely be reliant on the supplier in some way. This could cover areas such as hosting the platform, providing support, providing consultancy, and so on. Therefore, the firm needs to ensure

that the supplier complies with what they have committed to on the contract and appropriate service levels are agreed and in place along with a process for monitoring them. For example, are support calls being responded to per schedule? Are there issues with the hosting? And so on. If there are issues then these need to be escalated to senior management at both the supplier and firm.

- Change control process—IoT hardware and software will need to be added, updated, or removed. This could cover activity as part of the implementation project or part of business-as-usual running. Therefore, there needs to be a process to ensure changes are made safely to ensure existing functionality is not impacted adversely. Depending on the involvement of the supplier (such as hosting the platform), the supplier may need to be involved as part of this process.
- Policies for the development of IoT—Good standards need to be created around the development of bots. This will cover programming standards, integration standards, information security standards, testing standards, version control, and release procedures. Depending on the involvement of the supplier, the supplier may need to be involved as part of this process.

Ensuring the Firm has Sufficiently Skilled Staff to Support IoT Once the Project Completes

A dedicated project team will have been formed to implement the initial IoT project. This will have consisted of senior management to provide oversight and steer plus many "on the ground" people who would develop the software, rules, integrations, and so on as required. This group of people would have been sourced from in-house staff, contractors, and possibly staff from the external platform vendor if appropriate.

Therefore, firms must develop the necessary skills to be able to support the IoT platform once the project closes, because otherwise they will be reliant on external contractors and platform vendor staff.

This means that senior management will need to be educated on understanding IoT and its benefits at a general level.

Also more junior staff will need to be trained on IoT, the specific platform selected, the integration with back end systems as well as the suite of bots developed and rolled out as part of the project. This training can be done by training existing staff but it may also be necessary to recruit new permanent staff with the required skillsets.

Robust Security Must Be Implemented

There are some real challenges regarding security and IoT.

To allow IoT to work effectively then it will require data to be passed from the various remote IoT objectives (wearables, sensors, etc.) to a central back-end system for processing. This data could be related to personal data (names, addresses, etc.), payment details, balance details, customer service requirements, and other confidential data.

This means the IoT hardware and software must be secure, be able to cope with robust encryption, be impossible to tamper with and be able to combat viruses and other malware. If the firm owns the hardware and software (say as a sensor in branch) then this is possible by ensuring the relevant controls and governance is implemented. However, if the hardware is not owned by the firm (say a customer TV or watch) then this will create a challenge because the firm will need to support a range of different hardware each will differing operating systems. (This area is discussed in much depth under Self-Servicing in Chapter 6.)

There are various "horror" stories where hackers have accessed a firm's technology via inappropriately secured IoT devices. For example, a hacker gained access via the connection between a tropical fish tank and the firm responsible for maintaining the tank and its water quality.

The key point is that if people are nervous about security then they will not trust IoT and will not use it.

Social Acceptance of IoT

Like all new technologies, it does take a while for society to generally accept the new technology. This is true for IoT. Customers may feel uncomfortable having a device on them which is monitoring their behaviors, tracking their actions, and recording what they do (even if this monitoring is for the customers' benefit). In effect, it is a "big brother" worry.

Therefore, firms need to recognize this by being very clear and open on what the firm is using IoT for to ensure there is no confusion or misunderstanding. Firms also need to ensure that their customers are not materially disadvantaged if they do not use IoT functionality.

Power Supply Dependence

To allow IoT to operate successfully then all the remote devices (sensors, wearables, cameras, etc.) will need some sort of power source. This could be using the mains electricity, some type of battery or a newer type of power source (such as solar or wind power). The remote devices must have sufficient power to operate with backup options in the event of problems.

Remote Maintenance

The devices used to support IoT (such as sensors or cameras) will need to be maintained. This could be due to errors detected or due to the required hardware and software upgrades. These devices could be spread around the country, located in inaccessible places, or located in places that the firm does not own. Therefore, firms must have processes and procedures in place to allow for these devices to be remotely maintained quickly and efficiently.

Network Dependence

To allow IoT to operate then all the remote sensors, hardware, wearables, and so on will need a connection to the Internet to work, pass data, and so on. This connectivity could be via 4G, 5G, or local Wi-Fi. If there is no connectivity then IoT will not operate. Therefore, firms must ensure that Internet connectivity is in place with suitable backup contingencies in the event of problems.

Future Challenges

Table 9.1 The future challenges for IoT

Area	Details
Increased regulations	This area is neutral at the moment. At the moment, the take-up of IoT within Financial Services is still relevantly low compared to other technologies covered in this book. For this reason, local and global regulators are not looking to implement IoT-specific regulations at the present moment (although IoT is still liable to current regulatory demands around data protection, supporting customers, etc.). However, if the use of IoT increases within Financial Services or there are high-profile issues then the regulators will start to look to implement rules.
Changing nature of clients	IoT should have a good impact on clients. IoT will allow quicker and more convenient customer service through wearables and devices such as Internet televisions. IoT should also allow firms to collect data on customer behavior which will allow firms to improve their customer servicing, enhance product offerings, and allow internal efficiencies which will, in turn, provide cost savings and cheaper fees for customers. However, there are some issues that firms will need to manage carefully. Customers may feel uncomfortable having a device on them which is monitoring their behaviors, tracking the actions, and recording what they do. In effect, a "big brother" worry. Firms need to recognize this but ensure that customers are not materially disadvantaged if they do not use IoT functionality and also to be very clear on what the firm is using IoT for to ensure there is no confusion or misunderstanding.
Evolution of products	IoT should have a good impact on products IoT should allow easier, better, and more convenient product servicing through wearables and devices such as Intelligent televisions. IoT should also allow firms to collect data on customer behavior which will allow firms to enhance product offerings.
Lack of trust	This could be negatively impacted if the firm does not manage this area. Customers may feel uncomfortable having a device on them which is monitoring their behaviors, tracking their actions, and recording what they do (even if the monitoring is for the customers' benefit). Therefore, firms need to recognize this by being very clear and open on what the firm is using IoT for to ensure there is no confusion or misunderstanding. Firms also need to ensure that their customers are not materially disadvantaged if they do not use IoT functionality.

Accurate data	This area is impacted adversely. IoT needs very accurate data for its processing. If IoT is not passing or receiving data correctly from its remote devices then IoT will not work. Therefore, IoT means the firms need to ensure data is correct, timely, and accurate.
Poor operating and technology models	Operating models will be impacted negatively. IoT requires new technology, process, people, and so on to be layered on top of the existing complex and costly operating models. This will increase the overall complexity, cost, and risk of firms operating models.
Profitability/Cost drivers	IoT should be a benefit for firm profitability in the medium to long term. IoT will allow efficiency improvements which should reduce costs and increase profitability in some way. IoT allows firms to provide better customer servicing, perform cross-selling of products to increase revenue, and enhance products to also increase revenue. However, IoT does a large amount of money to implement. Therefore, it does require a sizeable implementation fee which will take a period to pay back.
Changing nature of the workforce	This area is neutral. While some staff will lose jobs because their roles have been replaced by IoT processes, there is the opportunity to learn new skills to support NLP going forward.
New competition and replacements	The impact here is neutral. Although IoT may be able to allow new competitors or entrants to move in the business slightly quicker and cheaper.
Risk profile	There is a negative impact on risk levels. While IoT has great benefits around reducing risks around customer servicing, operational efficiency, and internal risks (around fraud), this is massively out balanced with (a) the additional risks to the operating model and the need for correct data and (b) with the significant security risks where a firm's technology infrastructure can be accessed easily via an IoT device such as a vending machine.

Case Study

A large retail bank is using IoT technologies to monitor the number of people who use their branches. These sensors recorded how many people enter the branch, how many people left the branch because the queues are too long, how long the queues are, what requests the customers performed, and so on.

This monitoring has provided a wealth of data which has allowed the bank in question to manage customer servicing much more efficiently. This does not just cover opening (or closing) servicing booths but opening them at different times and creating specific service pods for specific common requests (such as paying in cheques).

Summary

IoT is a useful technology although its take-up is not that large within Financial Services. This is probably because IoT is more suitable for other industries such as physical manufacturing which would use IoT for monitoring machinery and factories.

However, if it is implemented then it will provide benefits around customer servicing, enhanced products, internal operational efficiencies, cost reductions, and revenue increases. But there are some challenges around IoT increasing the complexity, cost, and risk of a firm's operating models and putting more pressure on firms to manage data well.

Like all technology, the rollout of IoT does need some thought and focus. Therefore, firms will need a clear business reason for implementation. This should be supported by designing a robust IoT infrastructure covering the actual technology but also the required processes, skills, and oversight required. To further reduce the risk profile then IoT should be rolled out on a gradual basis.

Finally, there is a social acceptance challenge. Customers may feel uncomfortable having a device on them that is monitoring their behaviours, tracks their actions, and recording what they do. In effect, a "big brother" worry. Firms need to recognize this but ensure that customers are not materially disadvantaged if they do not use IoT functionality and also to be very clear on what the firm is using IoT for to ensure there is no confusion or misunderstanding.

CHAPTER 10

Trend 6—Natural Language Processing

Introduction

What Is Natural Language Processing?

Natural language processing (NLP) is a subset of artificial intelligence that is focused on programming computers so they can (a) understand the human language from a variety of inputs such as e-mails, instant messaging, written communications, and verbal which can then be processed by other systems as well as (b) producing natural language outputs again across various sources such as e-mails, written communication and verbal.

The benefits of NLP are widespread, namely:

- It allows firms to process a large amount of activity (such as customer queries or instructions) very quickly or even instantly without the need for having teams of people to assess the request and process it manually. This in turn improves customer servicing.
- NLP allows firms to be more scalable and cost-effective. Once they have their NLP infrastructure in place then it should be able to cope with a large amount of activity. If volumes increase then the infrastructure can be extended which is much cheaper and quicker than employing more and more staff.

NLP should not be confused with Neuro-Linguistic programming. They both use the abbreviation NLP.

The Three Main Types of NLP

There are various streams to NLP, but for this book they have been grouped into three main areas:

Speech Recognition

This involves converting human speech into some sort of computerized coding so business rules can be run against it.

For example, a customer telephones a call center, and they are met with an NLP agent. This agent will "speak" to the customer regarding what they want to do (such as checking a balance or making a cash transfer) and then interpret the request and then process the request as necessary. A second example is where an NLP program will review telephone recordings against a set of phrases (called lexicons) to determine whether any fraudulent activity may have taken place. If a match is found then it does not mean that there has been an offense but it will allow a warning to be raised so it can be investigated by the relevant human team.

There is a further development in this area which at the time of writing (winter 2021) is still fairly new and has not been rolled out by many firms. This relates to NLP agents being able to recognize the caller by speech recognition. Therefore, when a customer calls a contact center then the NLP software will authenticate the customer by their voice as opposed to using passwords, PINs, mother's maiden names, and so on. The obvious advantage is the whole process is quicker, easier, and more customer-friendly but there are some disadvantages. The technology is fairly new and it can struggle with people with similar voices and people who have an illness that impacts their voice. Also, there are unclear legal implications of using voice recognition to identify a caller. Finally, people may feel uncomfortable that they have identified themselves by entering a password or PIN.

Natural Language Understanding

This is developing software that will allow the system to read text or, in effect, allow computers to "read" albeit in some limited manner. The NLP program will receive in some written text (say from an e-mail, chat message, or document) which it will then review against a set of phrases (called lexicon) to try and understand what is being communicated.

For example, the millions of messages within a chat channel could be "read" instantly to determine whether any criminal activity is taking place. The NLP program will look for lexicons along the lines of "fix the price," "make sure legal do not know," and so on. As with Speech recognition above, irrelevant items could be identified because the system will review text literally. Therefore, a human team must review the outputs before any action is progressed.

Natural Language Generation

This is in the way the complete opposite of the above two. The NLP software will take the output of some type of process and produce natural language output. This could be the form of verbal communication (such as part of a call center), e-mail, instant message, written communication, or anything else. The outputs could consist of standard phrases (such as "Thank you [CALLER] for contacting us") or more complex constructed sentences that are dependent on circumstances.

How Does NLP Work?

Speech Recognition and Natural Language Understanding Work in a Similar Manner

Both these are very similar in concept. They both receive in some sort of human language message (either verbally or written) which needs to be translated so the computer system can "understand" it and process the request accordingly.

The process can be summarized with the three sequential stages below:

Figure 10.1 NLP speech recognition and natural language understanding flow

The first stage is to try and understand the message. This will involve receiving the message and performing the following activity:

- Break the message into smaller parts so it is easier to understand
- Remove common words (or noise) that are not needed—for example "of," "the," "etc." and "is"
- Look to correct any spelling errors
- Look to enhance any abbreviations—for example, "txn" should be "transaction" or "a/c" should be "account"

Once the message has been understood and cleaned up then it is possible to try and determine the actual request is. This is unfortunately hard to do due to the wording of the request, understanding the context of the message, errors in the request, and so on. However, the message will be compared against a set of lexicons to try and determine what the request is. If the request cannot be determined positively then there needs some exception process to review them by a human.

However, if the request is understood then it can be actioned. For example, process the bank cash transfer or provide an investment valuation.

Natural Language Generation

This area works in the opposite to the above where the computer generates a natural language which is then communicated to a human.

The process can be summarized as follows:

Initially, the system will produce some sort of output from a normal process. This will typically include some sort of confirmation statement (e.g., confirmation that a bank transfer has been completed successfully) plus some communication-specific data (account details, amounts, etc.)

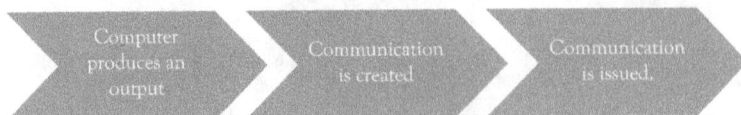

Figure 10.2 NLP natural language generation flow

This output is then converted into a string of words that will form the communication. This will consist of a set of sentences but checks will need to be made to ensure they link together correctly, have a natural flow, they are grammatically correct, and all technical terms are used correctly. Also, it may be possible to translate the message into different languages.

Finally, the communication is issued. This could be via the computer "speaking" over a phone, in a letter, on an e-mail, on an instant message, and so on.

Uses With Financial Services

There are a variety of uses for NLP with Financial Services.

Improved Customer Servicing

One of the most common uses of NLP is to improve customer service across contact centers, websites, and deal with customers' written correspondence (such as e-mails or letters).

Contract center telephone systems have been enhanced to allow customer telephone requests, e-mails, instant messages, written requests, and other requests to be processed by NLP. The system will "understand" the request and use a set of rules to either process the request or direct it to the correct area for processing.

In addition, the website has been enhanced with NLP functionality. This has allowed websites to support intelligent form filling or even auto-completion. It has also allowed better website searching because NLP will allow a better understanding of what the client is looking for and present the links they need. Finally, it has allowed virtual assistants (or Chabot's) to be installed which will allow customers to interact directly with the website which will "listen" and "respond" using NLP supported by a set of business rules and knowledge base to answer any questions or queries.

The end-result is that these improvements provide customer benefits because all requests are processed quickly and effectively. They also provide benefits to the firm because they do not need to employ large and expensive teams to process these.

Internal Efficiencies

NLP also allows internal efficiencies and cost savings.

All firms have clients and products across different jurisdictions and countries which means firms need to work with multiple spoken languages. Therefore, as NLP allows input and output communication to be processed automatically then it can also cope with different languages. This will save the need and cost of employing a team of translators.

In a similar vein, all firms have a vast amount of documents of which some could be many decades old. For example, firms will have mountains of client and supplier contracts often in paper or scanned format. Some of these contracts will have out-of-date clauses (e.g., around liability or indemnities) which could put the firm at risk. Therefore, NLP can be used to "read" these contracts and assess the suitability of all the clauses. Anything of concern can be assessed.

Fraud Management

NLP is being used to assess communications to determine whether any criminal and/or fraudulent behavior is taking place.

Inbound and outbound communications (e-mail, telephone recordings, trading messages, etc.) will be "listened to" by an NLP system against a list of known criminal and/or fraudulent phrases (or lexicons). Once the phrases are understood then they will be processed by a rules engine to determine whether they are fraudulent, criminal, or not. Anything suspect will be reported to the relevant teams. (These rules engines will typically be developed using Machine Learning techniques (see Chapter 7).)

A second example is where an NLP program will review telephone recordings against a set of phrases (called lexicons) to determine whether any fraudulent activity may have taken place. If a match is found then it does not mean that there has been an offense but it will allow a warning to be raised so it can be investigated by the relevant human team.

Product, Marketing, and Public Relations

Most firms receive a large amount of content. This cover market reports, newspaper, published articles, videos, interviews, trade journals plus many more. NLP allows this content to the "read" quickly to determine whether any new trends are emerging or whether the firm is being mentioned (especially if the firm is being mentioned poorly). This will allow the firm to take appropriate action.

Better Data Collection

One of the good side effects of NLP is that when an inbound communication is "read" and "understood," it is converted in a standardized format. This then provides a great source of data that can be used (by Machine Learning technologies (see Chapter 7)) to understand customer behavior, market trends, and so on. This will allow the firm to implement customer-servicing improvements, implement efficiency and cost-saving changes as well as many other possibilities.

Challenges of NLP

Ensure There Is a Clear Business Reason to Implement NLP

There are many stories of firms (not just in the Financial Services) implementing new technology for the sake of the technology as opposed to implementing technology to meet some type of business or strategic need. (In the same way as any major change) this means before embarking on an NLP implementation then a firm must have a clear business reason to implement the technology. Therefore, please refer to Appendix B which provides a checklist on the activities required when creating a Business Case.

Implement or Roll Out NLP in a Slow Phased Approach

One of the issues with NLP is that any issues can be very visible to customers and the outside world. For example, if a Chabot is not working or giving strange results then clients will see this immediately. This means that NLP must be implemented correctly.

Therefore, it would be sensible to structure the implementation plan around a phased approach. The initial phase would contain the implementation of the actual core platform but then there should be phases each containing a prioritized set of NLP. The prioritization should focus on the rules that are (a) easier to define and code and (b) the processes that offer the most business benefit. This approach will hopefully ensure the project delivers some immediate benefits which will create goodwill, momentum, and confidence. It will also help with financial payback and allow the firm to learn about NLP which could provide useful lessons for the future.

It is also important to understand what is needed to support the implementation. This could involve staffing such as senior management, operational staff, in-house technology staff, NLP platform vendor staff, technology staff who support the systems being integrated with, legal staff, compliance staff plus others. In addition, if the rollout of NLP involves staff losing their jobs (because their roles are being replaced by the new NLP technology) then these staff may need to be involved in the project. If so then this will require careful and tactful management.

Finally, it may also be necessary to ensure there is desk space for the team, test environments, shared document folders, e-mail lists, and so on.

Build a Robust Infrastructure to Support NLP

A robust infrastructure must be built to support NLP. This will cover (a) defining the end state, (b) implementing the new NLP technology and ensuring it integrates with the existing back end systems, (c) ensuring there are suitable controls and governance in place, and (d) the firms have sufficiently skilled people to support the infrastructure.

Defining the End State

NLP cannot be used for all inbound communications. Because essentially NLP uses a set of rules to determine what is being "said" then it will best with requests that are simple and easily codified. For example, asking for a balance, asking for a product document, requesting a transfer, and so on. NLP will not work well with complex requests such as a process the death of a customer, closing an account, or a very complicated complaint.

Although NLP can be generally used for most outbound communication on the assumption that the NLP systems can generate the grammatically correct outputs in the required languages.

Therefore, the firms must think clearly about the processes or functions that they would like to include within NLP. The best functions are those that can be codified easily and offer benefits to either (a) the firm in terms of risk management or efficiencies or (b) the client in terms of service improvements.

A Technology Infrastructure to Support NLP Will Need to Be Implemented

While it is fair to say that implementing NLP is not as complex and challenging as some of the other technologies in this book (say Big Data or Cloud Computing), it is still challenging.

For the inbound communications then the following will be required:

- A front-end will be required to receive the relevant communication such as website requests, e-mails, voice communication, or instant messaging. This front-end will almost definitely be part of a different system such as a contact center voice system, website, or e-mail server.
- This front-end will then "understand" the communication and pass it to a rules engine which will split up the communication into its relevant parts and then pass it to the relevant system for processing.
- The relevant (or back-end systems) will be an existing system (such as an administration or payment system) which will need to be enhanced to ensure it can process the message automatically.

The NLP front-end and rules engine is likely to be provided by an external supplier. It is possible to develop this technology in-house but it is simpler to purchase a package and then configure it. Therefore, the supplier must be selected carefully because once NLP is live and being used then this supplier will become a strategic supplier. Appendix A provides a list of the activities and areas to be covered when selecting a supplier.

Furthermore, the infrastructure (as in servers, networks, etc.) that will be supporting the NLP technology will need to be secure and robust. Remember that NLP is very visible to the external world and customers, and if problems are encountered then these will be seen by everyone. For example, if the contact center telephone NLP functionality is not working or unavailable then customers will notice immediately. This means that the infrastructure has sufficient resilience and BCP arrangements.

Therefore, some type of formal technology platform vendor selection process must be followed covering the points listed below:

Integration with Back-End Systems Will Be Challenging and Should Not Be Under-Estimated

While NLP is a very useful technology (especially if it is implemented correctly), it cannot work in isolation. When NLP "reads" in communication, it needs to pass some sort of message to another system for processing. Likewise, when NLP sends out a communication, it will need to be told what to say by other systems. Therefore, NLP cannot be implemented on its own and it will need to be integrated with existing systems.

Unfortunately, all firms often use legacy back-end systems built on older technology and supported by a combination of suppliers and in-house so implementing. This means that any integration would be complex and costly. Therefore, it will need careful design and planning from the start.

Ensure There Is Sufficient Governance and Control in Place Around the NLP Platform

As well as the implementation of the new NLP technology, new processes, and governance frameworks must be designed and implemented to control the new technology. This will cover four main areas.

- Oversight of the daily processes—Controls need to be in place to ensure the NLP application work as designed. If problems are identified then the cause needs to be discovered so both they can be fixed immediately. Any material issues will need escalating to management.
- Oversight of the supplier—The firm will likely be reliant on the supplier in some way. This could cover areas such as

hosting the platform, providing support, providing consultancy, and so on. Therefore, the firm needs to ensure that the supplier complies with what they have committed to on the contract. For example, are support calls being responded to per schedule? Are there issues with the hosting etc? If there are issues then these need to be escalated to senior management at both the supplier and firm.

- Change control process—Changes to NLP rules will need to be added, updated, or removed. This could cover activity as part of the implementation project or part of business-as-usual running. Therefore there needs to be a process to ensure changes are made safely to ensure existing bots are not impacted adversely. Depending on the involvement of the supplier (such as hosting the platform) then the supplier may need to be involved as part of this process.

- Policies for the development of NLP rules—Good standards need to be created around the development of NLP rules. This will cover programming standards, integration standards, information security standards, testing standards, version control, and release procedures. Depending on the involvement of the supplier then the supplier may need to be involved as part of this process.

Ensuring the Firm Has Sufficiently Skilled Staff to Support NLP Once the Project Completes

A dedicated project team will have been formed to implement the initial NLP project. This will have consisted of senior management to provide oversight and steer plus many "on the ground" people who would perform the developments, integrations, and so on required. This group of people would have been sourced from in-house staff, contractors, and possibly staff from the platform vendor.

Therefore, firms must develop the necessary skills to be able to support the NLP platform once the project closes, because otherwise they will be reliant on costly external contractors and platform vendor staff.

This means that senior management will need to be educated on understanding NLP and its benefits at a general level.

Also, more junior staff will need to be trained on NLP, the specific platform selected, the integration with back-end systems as well as the suite of bots developed and rolled out as part of the project. This training can be done by training existing staff but it may also be necessary to recruit new permanent staff with the required skillsets.

The Majority of Issues Relate to Understanding Inbound Communications

During implementation, the majority of problems will be trying to fully understand inbound communications. For example:

- There are many different ways to communicate the same request.
- Inbound communications are formatted differently. The same request will be formatted differently across voice, Chabot, e-mail, or written letter.
- Technical terms or abbreviations may be used incorrectly which could create confusion.
- There could be spelling errors, missing words, or grammatical errors.
- The same phrase could have different meanings.
- The communication could be across different languages. While is it possible to cover the main languages it will be impossible to cover the thousands of different languages around the globe.
- Voice inbound communications could have different accents or use local slang.
- People also tend to speak differently to a computer; for example: more slowly and exaggerated.
- People may use emotion in communications which may be hard to fully understand.
- People may also use sarcasm and/or satire.

Therefore, any NLP rules developed will need to be able to cope with the above.

There Are Still Some Challenges With Natural Language Generation

There are also some issues with outbound communications (although they are less challenging than inbound communication). For example:

- The NLP rules will need to be able to have sufficient vocabulary to be able to "say" what it needs to communicate.
- It will also need to be able to cope with all the different languages that customers may want to use.

It Is Important to Ensure Lexicons and Vocabulary Is Kept Up-to-Date

Firms must ensure that NLP lexicons (for understanding inbound communications) and vocabulary (for outbound communications) are constantly maintained to ensure they meet the needs of the system. There are several ways that this can be performed.

- Firstly, the supplier of the NLP infrastructure will maintain some type of list to which a firm can subscribe to.
- Secondly, it is possible to use machine learning techniques (see Chapter 7) to improve the inbound lexicons. This works in the following way. A machine learning algorithm will assess all inbound communications to determine whether there are any new or updated lexicons required. For example, are clients asking a product application form differently? This will then allow the relevant lexicons to be added to the NLP system and any appropriate rules. Also depending on the change then it may be necessary to update integrations with the back-end systems.

NLP Still Needs Some Social Acceptance by Customers and the General Public

There is an issue or challenge with the social acceptance of NLP.

Customers can be nervous with both (a) speaking and communicating to a computer or (b) a computer speaking or communicating back to them. Therefore, they will often stay on hold until they are passed to a human operator. This means firms still need humans in place.

Secondly, staff internally can be uncomfortable if they feel their activities are being monitored. In effect, some sort of "big brother" oversight. This means that firms need to be very clear about what monitoring is in place and why this monitoring is required.

Future Challenges

Table 10.1 Future challenges of NLP

Area	Details
Increased regulations	The impact is neutral at the moment. No specific NLP-related regulations have been implemented so far (apart from the existing regulations around ensuring operating models are robust, customers are looked after, etc.). However, if NLP becomes more popular and/or there are many major issues then the regulators may look to implement focused rules around NLP.
Changing nature of clients	The impact on clients is positive. NLP should allow customer servicing to be improved and to be run cheaper which in turn should allow for clients to be charged lower fees. However, there is a slight downside because some customers will be unhappy or uncomfortable "speaking" with a computer. Therefore, firms need to still ensure they provide a human to speak to if needed.
Evolution of products	The impact on products is positive. NLP allows products to be offered and serviced better and cheaper. Although the issues noted above regarding customers not wanting to "speak" with a computer will need addressing.

Lack of trust	The impact could be negative if not managed carefully. Customers can be nervous with both (a) speaking and communicating to a computer or (b) a computer speaking or communicating back to them. Therefore, they will often stay on hold until they are passed to a human operator. This means firms still need humans in place. Secondly, staff internally can be uncomfortable if they feel their activities are being monitored. In effect, some sort of "big brother" oversight. This means that firms need to be very clear about what monitoring is in place and why this monitoring is required.
Accurate data	This area is impacted adversely. NLP is very reliant on accurate data for processing inbound communications, building rules, processing outbound communications, and so on. If there are gaps, errors, and so on in the data then it will impact how well NLP can operate. Therefore, firms will need to implement more processes and rules around ensuring all NLP-related data is accurate.
Poor operating and technology models	This area is impacted adversely. While NLP does offer real business benefits, it does require another complex and business-critical component to be added into already existing complex operating models, thus increasing complexity and risk further.
Profitability/Cost drivers	This area is impacted favorably albeit in the medium to longer term. While NLP will improve efficiency as well as reduce costs and risk (e.g., around frauds), it does require a sizeable implementation fee which will take time to payback.
Changing nature of the workforce	This area is neutral. While some staff will lose jobs because their roles have been replaced by NLP processes, there is the opportunity to learn new skills to support NLP going forward.
New competition and replacements	The impact here is neutral. Although NLP may be able to allow new competitors or entrants to move in the business slightly quicker and cheaper.
Risk profile	There is a neutral impact on risk levels. While NLP will reduce risks around customer servicing, operational efficiency, and internal risks (around fraud), it is counter-balance with the additional risks to the operating model and the need for correct data.

Case Study

This case study relates to a global Asset Manager who used NLP techniques to analyze all their external contracts.

This manager had a large number of legal contracts. Some of them were recent and others were several decades old. Also, the actual contracts were spread over various formats (such as MS-Word, PDF, pictures, scans, paper copies, and microfiche).

The issue was that the manager did not have a clear understanding of all the clauses across the contracts. For example, what were the manager's commitments? what were the suppliers' commitments? what are the termination clauses? what liabilities are in place? plus others. Therefore the manager had no real understanding of their legal risk.

The manager decided to use NLP to try and address this problem, namely:

- A list of questions that needed to be answered and a list of terms that needed to be included was created. In effect, a list of lexicons was created.
- Soft copies of each contract were created. These were mainly PDF scans.
- Using an NLP application, all the soft copies of the contract were reviewed against the list of questions and the list of terms that needed to be included.
- The system then produced an assessment of each contract. If the contract covered the errors then it was assessed as Green. If it was missing some errors then it was assessed as Amber. Otherwise, it was marked as Red. (This assessment was run a few times because several problems were discovered with the lexicons which had to be fixed.)
- The list was then passed to a human lawyer for formal review. A number of the Green contracts were sample-checked to ensure the NLP assessment was working. All Amber and Red contracts were assessed in detail.

While a large manual or human effort was required, the NLP rules dramatically reduced the timeline and cost required for the initial assessment from several months down to a couple of weeks. This allowed the firm to focus its legal teams on the high-value work of actually changing the contracts.

Summary

NLP is a useful technology that provides benefits around customer servicing, operational efficiency, internal controls, reviewing documents, and providing standardized client data.

However, the complexities and challenges of implementing NLP must not be under-estimated which means firms will need a clear business reason for implementation. This should be supported by designing a robust NLP infrastructure covering the actual technology but also the required processes, skills, and oversight required. To further reduce the risk profile then NLP should be rolled out on a gradual basis.

Finally, there is an issue or challenge with the social acceptance of NLP. Firstly, customers can be nervous with both (a) speaking and communicating to a computer or (b) a computer speaking or communicating back to them. Therefore, they will often stay on hold until they are passed to a human operator. This means firms still need humans in place. Secondly, staff internally can be uncomfortable if they feel their activities are being monitored. In effect, some sort of "big brother" oversight. This means that firms need to be very clear about what monitoring is in place and why this monitoring is required.

CHAPTER 11

Trend 7—Digital Currency

Introduction

Digital currency is an area that is receiving a large amount of both good and negative attention at the time of writing (Winter 2021). However, like most new technologies and trends, one has to be able to separate the hype from the reality of what is happening.

What Is Driving the Movement Toward Digital Currency?

Digital currencies are part of the global trend of moving away from the traditional payment types (such as physical cash with coins/notes or cheques) to newer methods of payment (such as contactless payments). These methods are more convenient (i.e., one does need to carry cash around), are more secure (one does not need to write a paper cheque and post it), and do not require physical contact between payer and payee (which was exaggerated by the COVID-19 pandemic).

This trend has also been supported and aided by the following:

- Technology advances across the Financial Services industry and, in particular, banks, technology firms, and regulators.
- Increased government regulation and legislation to ensure that payment infrastructures are more robust and secure.
- Changes in customer behavior to stop using cash, cheques, and other more traditional payment methods. The key demographic tends to be the younger generation who are happy not to use cash. However, it is important to note that sizeable parts of society (especially older people) are still keen to use cash and, to a lesser extent, cheques for payments. This means that cash will be around for a while yet which means firms and society, in general, will need to support it.

- Increased standards globally across the financial services industry allows much quicker and safer payments as well as cheaper integration across payment technologies.
- Payment firms and providers are starting to merge into larger and more dominant firms which gives them the capacity and cost efficiencies to push out newer payments methods quicker and cheaper.

What Is a Digital Currency?

There are various definitions for digital or virtual or cryptocurrencies which mean trying to understand this area can be confusing to the layperson.

Therefore, at its basic level, a Digital Currency is any currency that is stored in a digital form. In other words, customer balances, transfers, and transactions are performed and stored on computer systems. The data could be stored in a centralized manner where there is a central book of records owned by a single organization (such as a Central Bank). Alternatively, the data could be stored in a distributed database (such as Blockchain) across its users with only its users being able to access it.

There are two main types of digital currency, namely:

- A Central Bank Digital Currency (CBDC) is a currency issued by a central bank. For example the EU's European Central Bank (ECB), the UK's Bank of England (BOE) or the U.S. Federal Reserve System (Fed).
- A virtual currency is a currency that has been issued by an organization or body that is not a Central Bank. (Sometimes virtual currencies are referred to as Crypto-currencies to reflect that their storage and usage are highly encrypted.)

Both of these are explored in more detail below:

Central Bank Digital Currencies

As mentioned earlier, a CBDC is a digital currency that employs technology to record a country's official currency in a centralized digital format.

The centralized storage would be managed, overseen, and underwritten by a single party such as the relevant country's central bank or financial regulator. CBDCs are sometimes referred to as Digital Base Money or Digital Flat Currency.

It is important to note CBDCs are not digital copies of a country's existing currency but they are part of the base money supply and a currency in their worth. While there has been a large amount of discussion regarding CBDCs, the actual rollout globally has been slow.

The advantages of CBDCs are as follows:

- Customers can use them very quickly over devices such as websites, mobile devices, wearables, tablets, and any other IoT device (see Chapter 9). Balances are real-time and payments/transfers can be made instantly.
- Because the currency is digital then it removes the need to carry large amounts of cash (i.e., notes and coins) around.
- CBDCs are cheaper to operate (because there is no physical cash to account for) which means payments both domestically and internationally are much cheaper and customers are charged lower fees.
- CBDCs are better at combatting fraud because all movements, transfers, balance inquiries, and so on can be tracked much easier.
- Finally, CBDCs can operate on a 24-hour day 365 days-per-year basis because there is no need to move or administer physical cash.

However, there are several disadvantages for CBDCs, namely:

- The roll-out of CBDCs is very slow at the moment and it is unclear which countries will roll out CBDCs soon. At the time of writing (December 2021), only five countries have issued CBDCs although another 14 are performing pilot investigations.
- CBDCs are entirely reliant on a single central data store. Therefore, if the central hub has problems or completely fails

then the relevant Central Bank cannot fall back or rely on
traditional paper money and coins.

• Finally, CBDCs often require special software to operate
which most organizations and individuals may not have
access to.

Virtual Currencies (Including Crypto-Currencies)

A virtual currency is any type of unregulated digital currency that has not
been issued or is controlled by a central bank. Examples are Bitcoin, Lite-
coin, and XRP. These currencies are controlled by the technologists who
created both the currency and the technology that underpins it. These
currencies are often only used by a unique group or set of customers.

Unlike CBDCs, virtual currencies are not underwritten by a central
bank or any other organization. For these reasons, they are sometimes
referred to as closed currencies or (less friendly as) functional currencies.

Although like CBDCs, virtual currencies can be centralized (where
there is a single central record of balances and activity) but most of them
are decentralized. Decentralized currencies are where a distributed or
decentralized technology is used to verify transactions and movements
across the user base. The most common or well-known decentralized
technology is Blockchain. This is a network that links records (or blocks).
When a transaction is requested then this request is sent to all the computers on the network for verification. If the request is approved then a
permanent and unalterable record (or block) is added to the Blockchain.
If the request is rejected then no updates or changes are made. The key
advantage of Blockchain is that it is not centralized which means (unlike
centralized databases) it is impossible to "hack" into and change in a
fraudulent manner.

The advantages of virtual currencies are as follows:

• Customers can use them very quickly over devices such as
websites, mobile devices, wearables, tablets, and any other IoT
device (see Chapter 9). Balances are real-time and payments/
transfers can be made instantly.

- Virtual currencies can operate on a 24-hour day 365 days-per-year basis because there is no need to move or administer physical cash.
- Because the currency is digital then it moves the need to carry large amounts of cash (i.e., notes and coins) around.
- Virtual currencies (and in particular Crypto-currencies) allow anonymity when processing transactions. While it could be seen as a good thing for the customer (especially if they want to keep their identity secret) it has led to claims that these currencies are being used for criminal activity.
- Finally, a virtual currency can operate on a 24-hour per day 365 days-per-year basis because there is no need to move or administer physical cash.

However, there are several disadvantages for virtual currencies, namely:

- The lack of regulation (from an independent third party) means there is a possible higher chance for virtual currencies to be used for criminal activity (such as Criminal Proceeds, Money Laundering, or Tax avoidance).

  Also, this lack of regulation poses problems for local and international regulators because (a) they cannot track their usage, (b) they do not understand the impact they are having on monetary policy, (c) they cannot ensure there is suitable protection around payments infrastructure and finally, and (d) they cannot ensure there are suitable consumer protections in place.
  At the moment, it is unclear how the regulators will react to these currencies. They could implement initial light regulation that may have a very little material impact but, alternatively, they could impact heavy and complex regulation which could make the currencies costly and complex to use or even completely unusable.

- The price of virtual currencies is very volatile with large price swings. While price increases are normally received well, there are often nasty shocks if the prices drop dramatically.

- The take-up and usage of virtual currencies by major stores and online websites is low because suppliers and customers would still prefer to use "traditional" payments methods of cash and credit cards. Also, some users and shops have complained that it can several minutes for a virtual currency transaction to process.
- Virtual currencies require specialist software to operate which most organizations and individuals may not have access to.
- Finally, while being decentralized does its advantages, it does have its own set of issues. The entire infrastructure is reliant on a collection of PCs, tablets, and other devices. Any issues with these could cause issues.

Uses With Financial Services

In theory, digital currencies can be used for any payments that are currently performed by existing "traditional" methods as long as both the payer and payee can accept the currency and have the necessary technology infrastructure in place.

Challenges of Digital Currencies

The Future Is Unclear Which Means Firms Will Struggle to Plan for It

The future for digital currencies is very unclear at the moment which is very challenging for firms to plan for this.

Regarding CBDCs, there is a lot of talk and discussions about what could happen. At the time of writing (Winter 2021), only five countries have issued CBDCs although another 14 are performing pilot investigations. This means that firms cannot allocate people, money, and effort into developing products and enhancing their operating models to support the rollout of CBDCs. Even if more CBDCs were launched then it is unclear whether customers will want to use CBDCs unless forced to by national central banks and/or regulators. People may still want to use the traditional currencies as they do now.

Virtual currencies are better defined because there are more currencies already up and running with a large number of users. However, their take-up is still relatively low and it is unclear whether the public will start to use them more or has their growth stalled. Also, there is a risk that if national authorities start to regulate virtual currencies heavily then it could make them less attractive to users which means they (or at least some of them) could become redundant. Therefore, and similar to CBDCs above, firms cannot allocate people, money, and effort into developing products and enhancing their operating models to support the virtual currencies because of this massive amount of uncertainty.

This means it is very much a case of a "wait and see" approach to see how the marketplace develops.

Digital Currencies Could Impact Existing Industry Models and Firms Will Need to React

While most people and organizations in the Western world will have several bank accounts, there are millions (or not billions) of people in other parts of the world who do not have a bank account.

Therefore, if digital currencies (and particular virtual currencies) became popular and mainstream then these people who do not have bank accounts could use these currencies for their accounts as opposed to using the "traditional" banks. This will create new competition challenges for the existing banks. Taking this further: apart from not picking up new customers, this movement could result in firms' existing clients moving their accounts to the new digital currencies which could result in (a) a loss of clients and profitability, (b) a large number of cash outflows which could impact the firm's liquidity position and even their stability, and (c) reduce cross-selling opportunities.

Therefore, firms will need to rethink their business model to cope with this. For example, they may want to move around from traditional bank accounts and deposit holding and look to develop new products around advice and other value-added services.

The United States and Other Western Countries Could Lose Their Dominant Currency Positions

At the moment, the United States and other Western countries dominate the currency market in terms of safe currencies and trading. The dominance provides economic power.

However, if other countries issue a CBDC or a particular virtual currency becomes popular then it could take away activity from the United States and other Western countries' currencies which means they lose their economic power.

The United States and Western countries will need to plan for this. On the positive side, they could look try and ensure their currencies are popular by perhaps issuing their CBDCs. Also from a negative point of view, they could look to ban or implement tough trade embargos on countries issuing CBDCs that threaten them. Also, they could look to ban or heavily regulate any virtual currencies that appear to be a danger.

Firms will also need to plan for this. They will need to ensure they can process any new currencies but ensure the products are relevant and their operating models can cope. It may also be necessary for firms to set up offices and operations in the countries that are issuing the new digital currencies.

The Use of Cash Is Reducing but Some People Will Still Want to Use It

As mentioned earlier, there is a growing trend to move anyway from cash as a payment method but there are still people and customers who will want to use cash. These people will be nervous about completely abandoning cash and moving to digital currencies. Therefore, there is a certain amount of social acceptance required. Therefore, firms will need to support "traditional" cash for the foreseeable future.

Operating Models Will Become Increasingly More Complex

While the future of digital currencies is still unclear (see "Challenges of Digital Currencies" on page 144), firms at some point will need to be able to process a range of new CBDCs and virtual currencies. This will be in addition to the existing "traditional" currencies that they currently support.

Therefore, firms will need to add components to their operating model to cater for this. This will involve adding in technology changes to be able to cope with accounting, payments, and so on for each of the individual digital currencies. (Bearing in mind that each digital currency operates differently then it will mean a large number of individual technology changes required although some sort of shared standards may develop over time.) These technology changes will need to be supported by new processes, newly skilled staff, as well as relevant oversight and risk control measures.

This will involve present legal and regulatory changes. Some virtual currencies are anonymous which will present real challenges for firms when trying to process their Know Your Customer (KYC) or Anti-money Laundering (AML) checks. This means some firms may not be able to support these currencies because they will not be able to perform these checks.

Future Challenges

Table 11.1 Future challenges of digital currencies

Area	Details
Increased regulations	This area will be impacted in a major way. Virtual currencies by nature are unregulated and are controlled by the developers or people who created them. There is no underwriting or external oversight by an independent third party. However, if regulators become worried about these currencies then it is not unreasonable to expect new rules to be implemented. This could range from light-touch rules which have no material impact, to complex rules that could limit the use of the currency. Similarly, if a CBDC is issued then it will be issued by a central bank and will come with a set of rules and regulations that users and firms will need to follow. The result is that firms will need to follow another set of regulations.
Changing nature of clients	The impact on this area is neutral. There is a general trend within society to move away from cash and cheques to digital currencies but this trend is being driven by the younger demographic. There is an older demographic who will be uncomfortable with not using cash (i.e., coins and notes) and therefore the industry will still need to support this.

(Continued)

Table 11.1 (Continued)

Evolution of products	The impact on this area is neutral. As digital currencies are rolled out and their usage increases then firms will need to ensure their products can cope with these currencies. This could cover bank accounts, investments, foreign exchange, insurance plus others.
Lack of trust	This area is challenging to predict. Virtual currencies started because of a lack of trust in national Governments and big firms (especially Banks after the Credit Crisis of 2009). Therefore, if these currencies are heavily regulated or a CBDC is launched that undermines virtual currencies then it could be perceived as the Government and/or the Financial Industry protecting itself at the expense of the customer and driving out competition. However, if virtual currencies are not regulated sufficiently and issues are encountered (such as customers losing money or there are dramatic drops in value) then the Government and/or Financial Services industry could be accused of not protecting customers sufficiently. This is an area that will change and will need monitoring by firms.
Accurate data	This area will be impacted adversely. Because currencies will be held digital then it is important that they are recorded accurately and any issues, errors, gaps, and so on are identified instantly so they can be escalated and addressed quickly.
Poor operating and technology models	Operating models will be impacted adversely. Firms will need to add components to their operating model to cater for any new digital currency that it needs to support. This will involve adding in technology enhancements to be able to cope with accounting, payments, and so on for each of the individual digital currencies. These technology changes will need to be supported by new processes, newly skilled staff, as well as relevant oversight and risk control measures. There will also be legal and regulatory challenges. Some virtual currencies are anonymous which will present real challenges for firms when trying to process their Know Your Customer (KYC) or Anti-money Laundering (AML) checks. Some firms may not be able to support these currencies because they will not be able to perform these checks.

Profitability/Cost drivers	If digital currencies become mainstream then it will impact the cost and revenue profiles of Firms and their bottom-line profitability. From a revenue point of view, new and existing customers may decide to use CBDCs and/or virtual currencies for their banking and payments needs. Therefore, they may decide to close their bank accounts which will reduce firms' income and cross-selling opportunities. This means that some firms may need to develop their business offering and move away from traditional bank accounts and deposit holding and look to develop new products around advice and other value-added services. From a cost impact, firms will need to enhance their operating models and products to support digital currencies. This will require an investment of cash and effort which may not be covered by a similar revenue increase.
Changing nature of the workforce	No material impact to this area although there will be opportunities for staff to learn about digital currencies allow the required operating model and product changes to be made.
New competition and replacements	This area will have a good impact on new entrants but could cause issues for existing firms in the marketplace. While most people in the Western world have bank accounts, many people in other parts of the world do not have bank accounts. Therefore, if there were suitable digital currencies then these people may use these for banking and payments needs, and not use the traditional banks. This means that firms will not generate revenue from these people. Also, this could mean that existing customers close their accounts and move to digital currencies. As mentioned earlier, some firms may want to move away from traditional bank accounts and deposit holding and look to develop new products around advice and other value-added services. At a more national or holistic level, the United States and other Western counties dominate the currency market in terms of safe currencies and trading. But if other countries issue a CBDC or a particular virtual currency becomes popular then it could take away activity from the United States and other Western countries' currencies which means they lose their economic power. The United States, Western countries, and firms will need to plan for this.

(Continued)

Risk profile	There will be a major increase in the risk profile caused by digital currencies.
	Initially, firms will need to enhance their already stretched operating models, at a cost, to support a range of differing digital currencies.
	Secondly, the introduction of digital currencies could cause a loss of new accounts and existing clients. This will impact revenue figures and could force firms to reshape parts of their business to focus on advice and value add activities.
	On the assumption that these currencies are regulated then there will be yet more regulation the firms will need to comply with.
	Finally, the rise of digital currencies could impact the United States and Western countries' dominance of Financial Services. Therefore, firms will need to ensure their products are relevant it may be necessary for firms to set up offices and operations in the countries that are issuing the new digital currencies.

Summary

Digital currencies are an emerging technology that could genuinely reshape a major part of the Financial Services industry.

At a bare minimum, firms will need to enhance their already thin and stretched operating models, at a cost, to support a range of differing digital currencies. This will cover implementing new technology, upgrading processes, ensuring staff are suitably skilled and reviewing existing legal arrangements.

While regulations around digital currencies are generally light, it is safe to say that if their popularity and use increase then the amount of regulation will increase which will create costs and further overheads for firms to comply with.

Also, the introduction of digital currencies could result in a loss of new accounts and existing clients. This will impact revenue figures and could force firms to reshape parts of their business to focus on advice and value added activities.

Finally, the rise of digital currencies could impact the United States and Western countries' dominance of Financial Services. Therefore, firms will need to ensure their products are relevant it may be necessary for firms to set up offices and operations in the countries that are issuing the new digital currencies.

CHAPTER 12

Trend 8—Cloud Computing

Introduction

Cloud computing (or "the Cloud" as it is sometimes referred to) is another emerging technology trend that is constantly mentioned which, while it does have many massive benefits, is complex to implement and support.

What Is Cloud Computing?

Cloud computing is an on-demand computing resource covering data storage and processing power. The theory is that a firm just pays for the storage and/or processing used without the need and fixed cost of an in-house complex infrastructure. It is similar in concept to pay-as-you-go utilities where the customer "turns on the tap" and only uses and pays for the water used (as opposed to having their in-house fixed cost water plant).

A cloud provider will have built a large, robust, and shared computing infrastructure. This will have massive processing power, solid resilience/BCP, and a massive amount of disk storage. Connectivity is typically provided over the Internet. The provider can then divide this infrastructure into segments or containers (using tools such as virtualization) for each firm. The containers can be expanded or reduced depending on firms' demands.

The advantages to the firm are that they do not have to support and maintain an infrastructure with associated fixed costs, technology complexity, and the overheads of having staff to support upgrades, monitor the infrastructure, deal with issues, and so on. While there are many challenges (see below), in effect everything is handed over to the Cloud provider to run with the cost model being moved to a variable basis which can match the firm's activity much closer.

There are a variety of service models and care is needed when selecting the model to ensure it meets the business need.

- Infrastructure as a service (IaaS): The cloud provider will offer the basic infrastructure such as network connectivity, servers, storage, and processing power. However, the firm will be expected to implement and support the cloud themselves. For example, installing the operating system, installing the applications, running upgrades, overseeing security, performing back-ups, and so on. Therefore, the firm has the advantage of not running the infrastructure but will need still need to support the operating system and applications.
- Platform as a service (PaaS): The cloud provider will provide the infrastructure (as IaaS) but will also support the operating system, manage security, and perform backups. The firm will still be responsible for installing and maintaining any applications.
- Software as a service (SaaS): The cloud provider will provide and support the infrastructure (per IaaS), the operating system (per PaaS) but they will also provide and support all the application software. The firm is consequently not responsible for supporting any of the infrastructure, operating systems, security, backups, and applications.
- Mobile "backend" as a service (MBaaS): This is a cloud computing platform that allows mobile applications (such as phones, tablets, and IoT devices (see Chapter 9)) to be able to access a back-end technology without the need to implement a complex and costly infrastructure.
- Function as a service (FaaS): This cloud provider will provide and support a platform that will allow firms to develop software themselves without the need for building and supporting a complex and costly infrastructure.

(IaaS, Paas, and SaaS are at the time of writing (Winter 2021) the most commonly used service models).

Cloud computing can also be deployed in one of three ways:

- Private cloud (sometimes known as an Internal or Corporate Cloud): This is where the cloud built is solely dedicated to a single firm. The advantage is that the firm has sole control over the cloud and cannot be impacted by other cloud users. However, the costs for running this tend to be higher because it cannot take advantage of a shared infrastructure.
- Public cloud: This is where the cloud is used by multiple firms. The advantage is that the costs are lower because the firm is sharing the infrastructure but there are issues around security with other cloud users and being impacted by other cloud users.
- Hybrid cloud: This deployment model covers a combination of approaches where configuration could consist of in-house infrastructure, private clouds, and public clouds. The advantage of this model is it removes the need and cost to migrate all applications to the cloud but this model can be very complex and costly to support. It is not that uncommon for firms to use this as a part of a phased implementation as they are looking to migrate all their applications to either a private or public cloud.

Uses of Clouding Computing Within Financial Services

The usage of Cloud Computing is growing within Financial Services. According to IBM's 2020 "Banking on open hybrid multicloud survey," 91 percent of financial institutions are actively using cloud services today (or plan to in the next 9 months) which is double the figure from 2017.

There are two main uses of Cloud Computing within Financial Services.

Migrating In-House Data Centers to the Cloud

Firstly, many firms are moving their traditional data centers (which were traditionally hosted either internally or with a specialist external provider) into the Cloud. These have been driven by cost savings, greater reliability, access to perceived unlimited data storage, access to perceived unlimited processing power, and the removal of the overheads of running a data center (covering upgrades, back-ups, and disaster recovery).

Lots of Suppliers and Service Providers Using Cloud Computing

Secondly, many firms are being forced to use Cloud computing because many of their providers and suppliers are moving their technology onto the Cloud. For example, various trading platforms and software vendors are moving their deployment onto the Cloud and providing a common set of APIs for passing trades into the system and for requesting data extracts from the system.

Challenges of Implementing and Using Cloud Computing

Have a Clear Business Reason to Implement Cloud Computing

As with a large number of the technologies covered in this book, there are many stories of firms implementing new technology for the sake of the technology as opposed to implementing technology to meet some type of business or strategic need. Therefore (like any big change), this means before embarking on any Cloud Computing implementation, a firm must have a clear business reason to implement the technology. Please refer to Appendix B for a list of the areas to be investigated when completing a Business Case.

Think About the End State Before Starting Any Expensive Work

Before embarking on the actual implementation then it is important to remember that implementing Cloud Computing is a challenging activity and it will require a large amount of pre-planning and a firm will need to have some sort of clear vision of how their technology infrastructure will look once the implementation has been completed.

The following key points need careful thought:

- How will the firm's technology infrastructure look once the project has been implemented? For example, what applications will move to the Cloud, what service model will be used and what deployment model will be employed (see above)?
- Once the list of applications to migrate has been agreed then it is important that the applications can run on the Cloud. For example, the Cloud deployed could have different operating system or database versions or have network delays which could cause issues with the applications' running.
- Also if any of the selected applications are supported by an external vendor then it is important to study any software licensing or support contract to ensure that the application is allowed to run in the Cloud. Some software vendors are not always keen on their applications running in the Cloud because they are worried that their software, source code, and/ or intellectual property will be stolen. It is not uncommon for software vendors to request further legal assurances before allowing firms to run their applications in the Cloud.
- It is extremely unlikely that a firm will be able to move all its applications into the Cloud which means proactive thought is required regarding what happens to the applications that are not or cannot be moved to the Cloud? These will need to be hosted either by the firm themselves or by an external data center provider. Thought will also need to be given to how these applications integrate with the applications moved to the Cloud and how Disaster Recovery could be run across the full range of applications.
- While it is not uncommon but some firms will have more than one Cloud provider, Cloud service models, or Cloud deployment models (especially if the firm consists of several acquisitions). Therefore, any integrations between them must be carefully thought about.
- Robust connectivity will be required between the firms' offices, the Cloud(s), and other data centers because if connectivity is lost then the firms will lose immediate access to all their applications. Sufficient backup communications lines will need to be in place and tested regularly.

Choose Your Cloud Provider(s) With Care

As the Cloud will support some (if not most) critical applications then a large amount of care and attention must be taken when selecting the preferred provider (or providers). Similar to many technology providers, the Cloud provider(s) will become a key strategic supplier.

Appendix A provides a list of the activities and areas to be covered when selecting a supplier.

Understand Where Your Data Is Being Held

One of the key benefits of the Cloud is that a firm will "hand over" its data and the issues associated with managing it to a supplier who will then store this data on a large robust infrastructure which is spread across many locations (for resilience and strength). However, having data spread around the world solves the problem of resilience but it creates material issues in ensuring firms comply with location data regulation.

Most jurisdictions will have their local or national data protection laws. For example, both the European Union (EU) and the United Kingdom (UK) have implemented General Data Protection Regulation (GDPR). The State of California in the United States has its California Consumer Privacy Act (CCPA). Japan has its Act on the Protection of Personal Information (APPI).

Therefore, when using a Cloud solution then the firms must understand and comply with these regulations. This means that the firm will need to ensure that the Cloud Provider(s) employed can comply with these regulations which will add more complexity, risk, and cost.

Security of the Firm's Data in the Cloud

The Cloud Provider will be holding a firm's data which means there will need to be sufficient and robust security measures in place. This will need to cover the following areas:

- Segregation of data between different Cloud providers' different customers. A firm would not want their data to be merged or accidentally contaminated with other users' data. Therefore, controls and processes need to be in place to ensure the data is not accidentally shared with other Cloud users.
- Sufficient encryption on the data held within the Cloud. Therefore, if the data was stolen or accidentally sent out then it would take a long time for the hacker to decipher it.
- Sufficient encryption on the communication links between the Cloud provider, the firm's offices, other Cloud Providers, data central, customers, suppliers, and so on. This will help ensure that if data is intercepted then it would take the hacker a very long to unencrypt it.
- Password protection to stop unauthorized access. This access would need to cover access to the data as well as access to the processes that control the data. For example, password controls need to be in place to allow certain users to create records, other users to amend records, and further users to view the data.
- Processes in place to immediately highlight, escalate and address any security issues. This means that in the event of a problem then it is immediately trapped so its impact can be assessed straightway and escalated appropriately.
- Ongoing robust oversight and governance of security processes need to be in place to ensure that the above is in place and constantly reviewed and updated for completeness.

Ensure That There Is Sufficient Oversight and Governance Is in Place for Living Running

Like all critical processes and vendors a firm will need to ensure that there is suitable oversight and governance in place to monitor the process when it goes into live running. This is essential because any issues or problems will need to be "trapped" immediately so they can be escalated and managed appropriately.

The areas that need to be covered are as follows:

1. Ensuring that all service providers are providing the services that they have contracted and committed to on a day-to-day operational level.

   This will cover the Cloud provider (or providers) but could also cover software vendors, network providers, running costs as well as any internal providers. This oversight can be provided by collecting regular performance metrics which can be combined into some sort of monthly report and overseen by a forum of relevant stakeholders. Any material issues or ongoing problems can be escalated and managed accordingly.

2. It would be advantageous to form some sort of senior management forum between the firms and the Cloud provider.

   This would act as an escalation point for operational issues that need senior management support but it would also act as a long-term planning forum. The firm would make the Cloud provider aware of their long-term business plans (e.g., opening new offices or launching new products) so the provider can make necessary arrangements. Likewise, the Cloud provider would let the firm know about their plans (such as enhancements or new products) which may be interesting to the firm.

3. Thirdly, it will be necessary to conduct ongoing due diligence of the Cloud provider to ensure the provider is still fit-for-purpose.

   The coverage of this due diligence will be wide. It will cover reviewing any operational issues that are impacting performance but will also cover many other areas such as technology, processes, people, management, governance, risk management, finances, cyber-securities, the supplier's suppliers plus any other relevant areas.

4. Finally, the firm will need to ensure they regularly test Business Continuity Recovery (BCP) and Disaster Arrangements (DR) to ensure they work and are fit-for-purpose.

This testing can be viewed from two different points of view. Firstly, the firm will want to perform their testing and this will require the Cloud provider to be involved. Secondly, the Cloud provider will want to perform their testing and will need the firm to be involved and possibly review and sign off the tests.

Ensuring the Firm Has Sufficiently Skilled Staff to Support Cloud Once the Project Completes

During the implementation of the Cloud migration, a dedicated project team will have been formed. This will have consisted of senior management to provide oversight and steer plus many "on the ground" people who would perform the developments, integrations, and so on required. This group of people would have been sourced from in-house staff, contractors, and possibly staff from the platform vendor. Once the project is completed then this project team will be disbanded.

Therefore, firms must develop the necessary skills to be able to support the migrated Cloud platform once the project closes because otherwise, they will be reliant on external contractors and platform vendor staff.

This means that senior management will need to be educated on understanding Cloud and its benefits at a general level.

Also, more junior staff will need to be trained on Cloud, the specific platform selected, the integration with the applications not the Cloud, security implications, and any other as well as any other changes made as part of the project. This training can be done by training existing staff but it may also be necessary to recruit new permanent staff with the required skillsets.

Migrate to the Cloud in a Safe and Risk-Free Manner

As previously mentioned, migrating applications to the Cloud is not an easy process. Therefore, a firm must employ a thoughtful and pragmatic approach to migrating applications across. This can be split into the four following phases:

Figure 12.1 Cloud computing migration approach

What Needs to Be Done?

Before any actual implementation or migration work is started or even any planning activity is progress, firms must think deeply about what needs to be done to allow the firm to migrate from its current technology infrastructure to the future state defined (see above). This thinking can cover the following areas:

- What technology issues need to be addressed?

  For example, what applications are migrating?, what applications are not migrating?, are application changes required?, do any system integrations need enhancing?, what security issues need addressing?, where will the data be held on the Cloud?, what BCP/DR changes are needed? plus many other issues.

- What legal issues needed to be addressed?

  For example, contracts will need to be put in place between the firm and the Cloud Providers(s) but there could also be legal issues around existing application providers, ensuring compliance with data protection laws, ensuring compliance with financial regulation laws, and possible terminating existing arrangements if they are not required (such as terminating data centers).

  Finally, it may be necessary to either inform or ask for consent to migrate clients to the Cloud. If so then this will need to be factored in.

- Firms will need to build a capability to support Cloud computing.

  While this is covered in more detail (in "Ensuring the Firm Has Sufficiently Skilled Staff to Support Cloud once the Project Completes" on page 159 above), firms will need to ensure they have the sufficient skills and capabilities to support Cloud computing once the project is completed. Otherwise, firms will be very reliant on external contractors and suppliers.

- Finally, firms will need to ensure they develop the required oversight and governance processes to monitor the Cloud computing environment once it goes live.

  This is discussed in more detail (under "Ensure that there is sufficient oversight and governance is in place for living running" on page on 157 earlier) but it will cover ensuring the Cloud providers are providing the service that they have committed to, holding senior management forums to plan strategically, performing ongoing due diligence of Cloud providers, and ensuring BCP/DR tests are completed regularly.

Created a Phased Plan

Once this list of "things that need to be done" is completed above then these activities need to be sequenced into some sort of implementation plan.

Due to the complex and critical nature of migrating applications to the Cloud then it is strongly recommended that a phased approach is used for the migration. Using a "big bang" approach would be too risky for the firm. The earlier phases would focus on the less complex and less critical applications initially with all other applications being covered by later phases. Although it is not that uncommon for the first phase to only cover a single application and to be called a pilot migration.

The advantage of the phased approach is that it allows the firm to review progress at the end of each phase and make corrections for the next phase. For example, is the business case still valid?, were there unexpected technology issues?, were there any unforeseen legal issues?, is the firm still on track to develop its in-house capability to support Cloud computing?, does the sequence of application migrations need to be changed?, and so on.

Migrate or Execute the Plan

Once the phased plan has been designed then it can be implemented although it could change if issues are found as part of the review points mentioned earlier.

Day-to-Day Running

Finally, once the migration is complete then the firm will move to a steady-state with the above-developed governance and oversight processes.

People Are Nervous About Their Data Being Stored on the Cloud

Customers (and staff) may be nervous, unhappy, or uncomfortable with their personal and financial details being migrated to the Cloud. They may be worried about whether the data will be stolen, subpoenaed by foreign governments, or generally misused. Therefore, any client communication must be managed carefully.

Regulators Are Now Starting to Take a Real Interest in Cloud Computing

Unlike some of the other technologies covered in this book, financial regulators are now starting to take a real interest in Cloud computing. The reasons for this are probably because Cloud computing is becoming more and more mainstream across firms. In particular, the UK regulator (Financial Conduct Authority) has issued a large amount of guidance which can be summarized as follows:

- Legal and Regulatory Considerations: covering having a business case, ensuring the service is fit-for-purpose, ensuring regulatory compliance, and so on
- Risk Management: covering ensuring the implementation is risk reviewed, all legal risks are understood, all operational risks are understood and processes are in place for monitoring, reporting, and escalating breaches
- International Standards: Ensuring that if the supplier used is internationally based then they are compliant with all local regulations
- Oversight of the Service Provider: Ensuring there is sufficient governance and oversight of the arrangements
- Data Security: Ensuring data is protected and both the firm and supplier complies with the required regulations

- Effective Access to data: Ensuring the firm can easily access their data
- Access to business premises: Ensuring that firm can access the physical offices of the Cloud Provider to meet management, see their operations, and perform audits
- Change Management: Ensuring there are clear processes in place to make and test changes
- Business Continuity: Ensuring there are testing and robust arrangements in place to cope with the loss of the service
- Resolution: Ensuring there are arrangements in place to effectively manage any material or legal issues between a firm and the Cloud Provider
- Exit Plan: Firms need to ensure that they can exit the arrangement with minimal disruption to the operation and regulatory obligations

Future Challenges

Table 12.1 Future challenges of cloud computing

Area	Details
Increased regulations	This area is being impacted adversely. Financial regulators are now taking an interest in Cloud Computer and, in particular, the UK (the Financial Conduct Authority) has suggested guidance around the following areas: Legal/Regulatory Considerations, Risk Management, International Standards, Oversight of the Service Provider, Data Security, Effective Access to data, access to business premises, Change Management, Business Continuity, Resolution and Exit Planning.
Changing nature of clients	The impact on clients is generally positive. Cloud computing should allow customer servicing to be improved and to be run cheaper which in turn should allow for clients to be charged lower fees. However, there is a slight downside because some customers will be unhappy or uncomfortable with their personal and financial details being migrated to the Cloud. Therefore, any client communication must be managed carefully.

(Continued)

Table 12.1 (Continued)

Evolution of products	The impact on products is positive because Cloud Computing allows products to be offered and serviced better and cheaper.
Lack of trust	No real impact although moving data onto Cloud creates nervousness with the customer because they could be worried about their data being stolen, subpoenaed by foreign governments, or generally misused. Therefore, any client communication must be managed carefully.
Accurate data	The impact here is negative. While the structure and content of data will not materially change, it will be stored externally on a Cloud which creates extra risks and demands around security and encryption.
Poor operating and technology models	The impact in these areas is typically negative. While the theory of Cloud computing is that all data and applications are moved to the Cloud, this is rarely true. There are always some applications that cannot be moved to the Cloud (whether this is due to complexity, technology constraints, cost, or legal issues) Therefore, a firm will always need to support applications across Clouds and other data centers. This creates complexity and risk around the operating model as well as areas such as application integrations, BCP/DR, change management, and ongoing support.
Profitability/Cost drivers	Longer term Cloud computing does reduce operating costs which will improve profitability. It will also move costs from a high fixed cost model covering data centers to a more variable cost that matches activity. However, it is important to note that (a) Cloud computing is an expensive project to implement and will require a payback period, (b) there will be new overheads in terms of governance, oversight, and staffing to support it, and (c) there will also be the need, with an associated cost, to support applications that cannot be migrated to the Cloud.
Changing nature of the workforce	The impact here is neutral. While there will be staff losses because "traditional" in-house or external data centers will be removed but there are staff development opportunities in learning about Cloud computing and associated areas.

New competition and replacements	This area is negative to existing firms but positive to newer firms. Cloud computing does allow quicker and easier access to the industry because arrangements can be set up much quicker than the traditional data centers. This is good for new entrants but causes issues for existing firms.
Risk profile	This area is impacted negatively. While Cloud computing does reduce the cost and operational risks around running a traditional internal and external data center, it does create new risks around regulatory demands, increasing operating model complexity, security/cyber threats, and new market entrants.

Case Study

This case study relates to an Asset Manager who has a complex technology infrastructure with many different overlapping applications and multiple data centers (some in-house and others outsourced to vendors). This entire infrastructure was complex, costly to manage, and very challenging to make changes to.

Therefore, this firm looked to move their entire technology infrastructure into the Cloud. The perceived benefit was that it would make the technology infrastructure easier to operate, cheaper to manage, and much quicker and easier to change if required.

The firm completed a Cloud vendor selection process. This covered creating a list of possible suppliers, completing an assessment of each provider's capabilities, selecting a preferred vendor, completing contract negotiations (with due diligence), and then building a migration plan. This migration plan was phased with the initial focus on migrating noncritical applications first to test how well the Cloud works and learn lessons from the migrations. The later stages of the plan contained more critical and complex business applications.

However, as soon as the project started, the firm hit material problems. Some of the applications that were due to be migrated had technical issues with working on a Cloud-based environment. Also, some of the external suppliers who developed and supported these applications were extremely unhappy and nervous about their software being migrated onto a Cloud. Therefore, they insisted on strict legal demands to be included in contracts to protect their intellectual property.

If the firm had performed proper up-front assessment then these issues would have been highlighted so the implementation plan would have taken them into account.

The result is that the project ground to a standstill and at the time of writing (Winter 2021) these material issues are still outstanding.

Summary

Cloud computing is now becoming more and more common across the Financial Services industry. Its increased usage has been triggered (a) by firms migrating their traditional internal and external data centers to the Cloud with associated cost savings and (b) by the services being used by firms (such as trading platforms) being migrated to the Cloud by their providers. (As discussed above, the usage of Cloud Computing is growing within Financial Services. According to IBM's 2020 "Banking on open hybrid multicloud survey," 91 percent of financial institutions are actively using cloud services today (or plan to in the next 9 months) which is double the figure from 2017.)

However, migrating to the Cloud is not an easy activity and care must be taken.

There are a variety of possible service models (such as IaaS, PaaS, SaaS, MBaaS, and FaaS) and deployment models (such as Private, Public, and Hybrid). Each of these has its own set of distinct advantages and disadvantages.

Therefore firms need to have a clearly defined business case outline the business benefits (linked to the strategy of the firm), the costs required to implement Cloud computing, the potential costs savings as well as what the end state will look like (bearing in mind that not all applications will be able to be moved onto the Cloud).

Firms will also need to carefully select their Cloud provider to ensure they provide the required functionality, they have suitable costs, their legal contracts are acceptable, and (because they will become a strategic supplier) there is a good cultural fit between the firm and the provider.

Detailed thought and planning are then required around what needs to be done to perform the migration. For example, applications to be moved, applications that cannot be moved, changes to applications, security implications, oversight for live running, ensuring there are sufficiently skilled people within the firm, legal implications, client trust issues, and regulatory demands.

Once this is completed then a phased implementation plan should be followed to migrate the applications across in a secure and risk-free manner with regular review points to allow lessons learned to be implemented.

Finally, once this is completed then the Cloud is fully live.

CHAPTER 13

Trend 9—Big Data

Introduction

Big data is another one of the emerging technology trends that is receiving a large amount of attention, especially around what it can do, its challenges, and how it could make the world a better place. However, it is important to remember that, while Big Data does have a large number of positives, it does have its challenges which means the firms need to take careful care regarding its implementation and ongoing use.

What Is Big Data?

There are a variety of different definitions available of Big Data available but, at a general, Bug Data can be defined as:

1. There is a massive amount or volume of data. While volume and size of data are often relative to an organization's circumstances, we are taking in the range of millions (if not billions) of different data items which each data item often contains hundreds (if not thousands) of different variables.
2. The data itself is constantly changing often at a rapid pace. This means that new data items are being added as well as existing data items being changed or deleted.
3. The data is stored across a variety of different formats. This could cover the "traditional" structured formats such as databases (such as relational, No-SQL, or hierarchical), flat files, spreadsheets, XML lists plus others. It also covers many less structured formats such as video recordings, audio recordings, scanned documents, free format text, social media postings plus others.

With this data being collected then organizations can perform various types of data analysis. Historic analysis can be performed to determine the correlation between variables and data items, patterns of behavior, trends, and other themes. This analysis can then be used to (a) understand historic behavior, (b) predict future events or behaviors, and even (c) try and change future behaviors.

There is a clear link and dependence between Machine Learning (see Chapter 7), Cloud computing (see Chapter 12), and Big Data. Big Data will provide the underlying raw data that will allow Machine Learning algorithms to be developed, tested and executed using Cloud computing.

Generic Uses of Big Data

The section below outlines some of the uses of Big Data for Financial Services, but there are a variety of generic uses that are worth discussing.

- Local and national governments will collect a vast amount of data from their citizens regarding their age, health, lifestyle, and so on and then use Machine Learning techniques to create algorithms that will help understand what causes certain diseases and illnesses so governments can implement policy or legal changes to try and change people's behavior.
- Political parties have been using Big Data and Machine Learning techniques to try and understand what makes voters vote in a certain way or another. Once these are understood then political parties can then run very targeting campaigns to try and alter voter intentions.
- Similarly, meteorologists can use Big Data techniques to gather data on weather conditions and use Machine Learning techniques to create algorithms to try and predict weather patterns. These predictions can be provided to a range of areas such as airlines, ships, and so on.
- Finally, Big Data (again with Machine Learning techniques) can assist with the "normal" day-to-day functions of running a business. This could cover understanding what drives costs, understanding customer behavior, understanding what drives customer selling decisions, and understanding operational

efficiencies. This will, in turn, allow organizations to make changes to rectify these issues.

Figure 13.1 *Big data overview*

How Does Big Data Work?

At a high level, Big Data can be split into three sequential stages:

Data Gathering

This stage covers obtaining or gathering the required data that a firm needs to perform its analysis.

At a high level, there are two types of data:

- Primary Data: This is data that a firm has gathered first-hand or itself (typically as part of its normal business operations). For example, customer details, customer behavior, trading patterns, sales figures, operational costs, and so on. This can be sourced from a variety of sources such as application systems, Internet of things devices (see Chapter 9), or Natural Language Processing activity (see Chapter 10).
- Secondary Data: This is data that another firm or organization has collected which the firm in question has purchased or obtained in another way. This could cover data such as economic data, marketing data, demographic spreads, general market behavior, and so on.

A set of technology (with supporting business processes and controls) will be developed that will

- Consume the required data. This consumption could be real-time, ad-hoc, or regular.

- Clean the data. Even for the most accurate and robust data, there will always be issues such as missing attributes. Therefore, firms will need to review all the data received against a set of known controls then fix (or "clean") the data before it is sent further.
- Normalize the data. Because the (now cleansed) data has been received from a variety of different sources then it will be formatted differently. This could range from numeric fields being rounded differently to different date formats to different currencies. Therefore, all this input data will need to be converted (or normalized) into a single format that is suitable for storage.

Data Storage

Once all the data above has been gathered, cleansed, and normalized then it will need to be stored in some type of data storage. Because Big Data allows a wide range of data items to be held ("traditional" data records, videos, social media messages, e-mails, etc.) then the designated storage technology must be selected carefully.

As mentioned previously, organizations are now looking to move away from the traditional relational-type databases because they cannot support the volume, speed, and different types of data required for Big Data. This means organizations are now looking at technologies such as No-SQL and hierarchical databases. They are also looking to host these databases on the Cloud (see Chapter 12) because it avoids having complex and costly data stores running in-house.

Data Analysis

Once the data is being gathered and stored then it is possible to analyze this data for business advantage.

At the most simple level, it is possible to develop reports and outputs that perform simple but rather shallow analysis of the data. For example sales by region, operational errors by product type, revenue lost to fraudulent activities, and so on.

However, if Big Data is combined with Machine Learning then it is possible to generate much deeper and more useful analysis. While this is explained in more detail in Chapter 7, Machine Learning will allow organizations to uncover trends, behaviors, causes of issues, and so on that are not that obvious to the human eye. This will then allow organizations to improve their operating model, improve their risk controls, improve cross-selling, and so on.

Uses With Financial Services

There are many uses that Financial Services are using Big Data for (and the majority of these work in conjunction with Machine Learning).

Real-Time Stock Market Insights

Big Data (again working with Machine Learning) has helped with providing more accurate real-time stock market insights. Previously, it was only possible to analyze stock price, bond price, and exchange rate movements. However now with Big Data, it is possible to gather real-time data on political, micro-economic, macro-economic, and social trends which (using Machine Learning techniques) will provide more insight on how these impact stock price, bond price, and exchange rates. This in turn will allow firms to make better investment decisions.

Fraud Detection and Prevention

Firms are using Big Data to improve their fraud detection and prevention capabilities. Big Data has been used to collate vast amounts of information on customer behavior, market behavior, and environmental issues which will allow firms to predict what causes frauds. This allows firms to improve the processes and controls to either (a) prevent frauds and/or (b) be aware when fraud is taking place so suitable action can be taken.

Improved Risk Analysis

One of the biggest issues that firms are challenged with is managing the increased level of risk caused by their customers, the marketplace, regulation, and the general economy or environment. Big Data can help mitigate risks to a certain extent. Data on customer, market, and environment behaviors and how these contribute to or mitigate risks can be collated which will then allow Machine Learning techniques to be used to see what activities help or hinder risks so firms can change their operations accordingly.

Improved Customer Servicing and Selling

Due to the rise of Customer Self Servicing (see Chapter 6) and other automation then firms have a vast amount of data on customer behavior, their buying patterns, and their demographics. This data can be analyzed to determine what customer servicing improvements are required, what triggers selling decisions, and so on. This will allow firms to make operational improvements, target certain client groups for cross-selling as well as develop new or enhance existing products to make them more appropriate to the marketplace.

Operational Efficiencies

All firms have large, complex, and often disjoined operating models which leads to inefficiencies, errors, costs, poor customer service, and regulatory issues. Therefore, Big Data can be used to gather data on operational activity so firms can understand what is causing these problems so remedial action can be taken.

Financial Analysis

Similar to the section above, firms often have a complex set of costs that are hard to understand in detail. Big Data will allow firms to model their cost profile to try and understand what causes costs, what are fixed costs, what are step costs, what are variable costs, and so on. This understanding then allows firms to make changes to improve their cost profile.

Challenges of Big Data

As noted earlier, Big Data has several great benefits, but it is important to understand that implementing and using Big Data is not an easy activity and firms need to think and plan carefully about any implementation.

What Is the Business Reason to Implement Big Data?

There are many stories of firms (not just in the Financial Services) implementing new technology for the sake of the technology as opposed to implementing technology to meet some type of business or strategic need. (In the same way as any major change) this means before embarking on a Big Data implementation then a firm must have a clear business reason to implement the technology.

For example, what sort of analysis or insight is the firm looking to use Big Data for? This could cover items such as trying to improve trading patterns, reducing operational costs, understanding client behavior, reducing fraud, and so on. Each of these is different with different data requirements, challenges, and costs. Therefore, firms need to have a very clear understanding of what their business case is.

Please refer to Appendix B for a list of the variables to be discussed when completing a Business Case.

Clean, Accurate, and Timely Data Is Essential

While it is obvious to say that firms need clean, accurate, and timely data for Big Data, it is often an area that firms neglect because they are completely focusing on the "glamour" of implementing a Big Data hub with the related analysis and/or Machine Learning tools. However, if the data that is "fed into" the Big Data hub is poor then any "output" analysis will be flawed.

Poor data can be caused by a variety of reasons, namely:

- The data could be taken from a variety of different sources which are completely separate and challenging to link together. For example, the input data could be based on different assumptions, different date ranges, analyzed at a different depth, collected for a different reason plus many others.
- The data is of poor quality. This could cover gaps in the data, errors in the data, and data being presented differently (such as clean vs. dirty priced bonds). Apart from t causing problems with linking data sets together, this poor quality may result in dubious or even completely wrong outputs.

- The data may be gathered over an inappropriate sample size, which means the results could be biased and/or incomplete. For example, if a firm is looking to assess trading patterns then they should aim to gather data across all asset classes, all types of trades, all types of market volatility, and so on.

To be fair, it is somewhat naive to expect to have fully complete data with no gaps or errors in it. This means that firms will need to fully understand any gaps or issues in their input data so (a) relevant data cleansing can be factored into the pre-processing and (b) any suitable adjustments or even disclaimers to the outputs can be made.

Start Small and Then Grow Implementation

There is a clear tendency to try and implement new technology too quickly. This is because people get "carried away with the technology." This is especially true in Financial Services. However, implementing any new technology is a challenging process and it should be taken gradually with regular point reviews.

Therefore, it is normally advisable to perform some sort of pilot implementation to assess: does the technology work?, does it offer the benefits promised?, and does the firm have the skills to implement the technology? The results of the pilot study can inform the rest of the implementation. For example, how quickly should the roll-out be performed?, what skills are needed?, will Machine Learning provide the benefits promised?, and so on. It is not that uncommon for firms to considerable rethink machine learning projects after the pilot stage because the technology is more complex or costly than originally thought.

Even once the pilot study is completed then a gradual rollout plan should be implemented. This allows the firm to understand the technology and associated impacts as well as build confidence, momentum, and a return on investment with senior management.

Build a Big Data Technology Capability

This is a key decision because if the wrong or inappropriate technology platform is selected then it will cause issues during implementation and day-to-day working, which will ultimately cause the change to fail.

As discussed above (and repeated below for ease of reading) there are three technology elements to Big Data.

Figure 13.2 Big Data overview

While it is possible to develop an in-house technology platform to support Big Data, most firms will struggle with this due to the sheer volume of data, the different formats of data, and the speed that the data changes. This means that firms will look to an external supplier to provide the required technology. Typically, firms will use a Cloud Computing provider to provide the "Data Gathering" and "Data Storage" capability and use a combination of data analysis and Machine Learning tools for the "Data Analysis" requirements. Therefore, some type of formal technology platform vendor selection process must be followed. Please see Appendix A which contains a list of the checks to be performed when selecting a supplier.

Regardless of approach, Big Data is another operating model or technology component that will need to be plugged into a firm's existing complex operating models. This extra component will need to be supported by suitably skilled people, processes, and systems in conjunction with possible external suppliers. The result is that the firm's operating model's complexity, cost, and risk profile increase.

Ensuring the Firm Has Sufficiently Skilled Staff to Support Big Data Once the Project Completes

A dedicated project team will have been formed to implement the initial Big Data project. This will have consisted of senior management to provide oversight and steer plus many "on the ground" people who would perform the developments, integrations, and so on required. This group of people would have been sourced from in-house staff, contractors, and possibly staff from the platform vendor.

Therefore, firms must develop the necessary skills to be able to support the Big Data platform once the project closes because otherwise, they will be reliant on external contractors and platform vendor staff.

This means that senior management will need to be educated on understanding Big Data and its benefits at a general level.

Also, more junior staff will need to be trained on Big Data, the specific platform selected, the integration with back-end systems as well as the suite of bots developed and rolled out as part of the project. This training can be done by training existing staff, but it may also be necessary to recruit new permanent staff with the required skillsets.

Data Privacy and Data Security Regulations

Data privacy and security legislation is complex and hard to understand at the best of times (especially if firms operate across many legal jurisdictions). Most jurisdictions will have their local data protection laws. For example, the European Union and the UK both have General Data Protection Regulation (GDPR). The U.S. state of California has its California Consumer Privacy Act (CCPA). Japan has its Act on the Protection of Personal Information (APPI). There is also similar other regulation across the globe.

However, the level of risk and complexity will increase when firms implement Big Data. Firms must understand and comply with these regulations and ensure that they (and their suppliers) fully comply with these regulations. This will add more complexity, risk, and cost.

Ensure There Is Sufficient Governance and Control in Place

While Big Data offers good opportunities it does create several risks that need to be governed and controlled. Big Data infrastructures can be complex which is a danger is as firms become more and more reliant on them. Therefore, firms need to implement policies, controls, and oversight around Big Data to ensure its usage is controlled and understood. Any problems found should be escalated to senior management in the same way as any other risk or issue.

These controls need to cover four main areas.

- Oversight of the daily processes: Controls need to be in place to ensure the data is being gathered, stored, and analyzed as designed. If problems are identified then the cause needs to be discovered so its impact can be assessed and the issue fixed. Any material issues will need escalating to management.
- Oversight of the supplier: The firm will likely be reliant on the supplier in some way. This could cover areas such as hosting the platform, providing support, providing consultancy, and so on. Therefore, the firm needs to ensure that the supplier complies with what they have committed to on the contract. For example, are support calls being responded to per schedule?, are there issues with the hosting?, and so on. If there are issues then these need to be escalated to senior management at both the supplier and firm.
- Change control process: Data will need to be added, updated, or removed. This could cover activity as part of the implementation project or part of business-as-usual running. Therefore, there needs to be a process to ensure changes are made safely to ensure existing data and analysis are not impacted adversely. Depending on the involvement of the supplier (such as hosting the platform) then the supplier may need to be involved as part of this process.
- Policies for making changes to the Big Data infrastructure: Good standards need to be created around making changes. This will cover data standards, programming standards, integration standards, information security standards, testing standards, version control, and release procedures. Depending on the involvement of the supplier then the supplier may need to be involved as part of this process.

The Dark Side of Big Data and Social Acceptance

Big Data does sometimes receive bad publicity regarding how it has been used to change (or manipulate) people's behaviors to the advantage of somebody else. For example, making people buy a particular product or vote in a particular manner. (However, it could be argued that this is not necessarily a bad idea, because if Big Data is used to make people eat healthier or reduce traffic congestion then one could argue that this is good for society.)

However, this is something that firms need to be aware of because clients, staff, and society, in general, are nervous about organizations using Big Data techniques to manipulate them. This means that firms need a clear business reason for their use (see "What is the business reason to implement Big Data?" on page 175 above) as well as having strong governance controls regarding its use (see "Ensure there is sufficient governance and control in place" on page 178 above).

Firms will also need to be reasonably open regarding their use of Big Data in case clients or staff ask questions. If firms appear secretive or obstructive then it creates nervousness and tension.

Finally, while there is no specific Big Data financial regulation at the moment, this could change in the future. If Big Data becomes more mainstream and if there are several high-profile issues then it is expected that the relevant regulators will look to implement rules. These rules could areas such as firms clearly publicly stating what they are using Big Data for and what their governance controls are.

Does the Analysis Produced Sound Sensible?

While this point is covered in the Machine Learning chapter in this book (see Chapter 7), it is important to always double-check or even be skeptical regarding any analysis, trends, or insights generated. Because of the complexity around the amount of data, the different types of data, the constantly changing nature of the data as well as the actual challenges of analyzing it then there is a chance of issues.

Therefore, for this reason, it is recommended that multiple different models are developed using different development techniques. This will provide several models whose outputs can be compared to help highlight any issues.

Future Challenges

Table 13.1 Future challenges of Big Data

Area	Details
Increased regulations	The impact for this area is neutral at the moment. There is no specific Big Data financial regulation at the moment, this could change in the future. If Big Data becomes more mainstream and if there are some high-profile issues then it is expected that the relevant regulators will look to implement rules. These rules could areas such as firms clearly publicly stating what they are using Big Data for and what their governance controls are.
Changing nature of clients	The impact on this area is positive. If used appropriately then Big Data (with Machine Learning) will allow firms to understand their customer better which will allow them to (a) improve their customer servicing and (b) develop better products for the marketplace.
Evolution of products	The impact on this area is positive. Similar to client impacts directly above; if used appropriately then Big Data (with Machine Learning) will allow firms to understand their customer better which will allow them to develop better products for the marketplace.
Lack of trust	The impact in this area is mixed at the moment. While Big Data will allow customer behavior to be understood which will allow improvements in customer servicing and products to be made, customers can be nervous or skeptical about being monitored. In effect, they may see firms as a "big brother" overlooking them. Therefore firms need to be open about what they are using machine learning for and how it will benefit the customer.
Accurate data	This impact is impacted adversely. The running of Big Data is very reliant on timely, accurate, and complete data. If the data has issues then Big Data will not work. Therefore firms will need to implement technology, process, controls, and oversight to ensure all data used is as correct as possible with any issues being identified.

(Continued)

Table 13.1 (Continued)

Poor operating and technology models	This impact is impacted adversely. Big Data is another operating model or technology component that will need to be plugged into a firm's existing complex operating models. This extra component will need to be supported by suitably skilled people, processes, and systems in conjunction with possible external suppliers. The result is that the firm's operating model's complexity, cost, and risk profile increase.
Profitability/Cost drivers	Big Data should in the long term (at least) support firms in improving their profitability. Understanding customer behavior should allow better products, cross-selling, and improved customer servicing. This should stop customers from leaving as well as attract new customers. The result should be an increase in revenue. Likewise using Big Data to reduce risk events (such as fraud) and improve operational efficiency should reduce operating costs. However, it is important to note that Big Data will require a cost to implement as well as additional running costs. Therefore (as part of the business case), firms need to understand any payback period.
Changing nature of the workforce	The impact on this area is generally positive. Big Data requires new skills. This covers both understanding Big Data at a conceptual level and also understanding the technologies to develop and build models. This offers career development possibilities for staff. However, there is one possible downside. If Big Data is being used to improve operating model efficiency then there is a possibility that some staff could either lose or have their jobs change as a result.
New competition and replacements	The impact on this area is positive to the customer. This is because new and/or more agile firms may be able to use Big Data to develop more innovative, functionality-rich, and better products for customers. This is good news for customers but a risk for other firms.
Risk profile	The impact on this area is neutral. Big Data does create risks about another piece of technology that needs to be supported by an existing complex operating model. Also as vendor platforms are often used then the risk of supplier reliance increases as well. But if it is implemented fully then it will reduce risks around fraud, operating inefficiencies, poor customer service, and losing revenue.

Case Study

The case study relates to a large UK subsidiary of a large U.S. bank that had a very large retail customer base (i.e., several million customs) spread across the UK and mainland Europe.

Despite having a large number of clients, the firm did not feel that they understood their customers based on which customers were profitable, which products were profitable, and what their customer buying behaviors were. This meant they were not pushing profitable products, probably supporting unprofitable products and not taking advantage of cross-selling opportunities.

Therefore, this firm implemented a Big Data infrastructure to allow them to deeply assess their client base. The firm carefully selected a Big Data storage provider. They also diligently implemented data gathering interfaces (with cleansing and normalization) from all their client, banking, and trading systems. Finally, they selected and integrated a Machine Learning application which they used to generate analysis, reporting, insights, and trends.

This appeared to be working fine until it was discovered (by one of the firm's in-house legal team) that the Big Data platform was in breach of various data protection regulations and customer confidentiality clauses. Therefore, all reporting and activity on the platform was immediately halted while the firm investigated what changes needed to be made to address these problems.

At the time of writing, this investigation work is still in progress.

This case study stresses the importance of ensuring all regulatory and data protection laws are understood and taken into account in the design of a Big Data infrastructure. Big Data is not just about implementing technology.

Summary

Big data is another useful technology that will provide benefits to firms and their customers. However, like all technologies, thought is required around its implementation, and day-to-day running is required. Also, Big Data cannot do anything on its own. In effect, it is a large collection of constantly changing data covering multiple formats. This means Big Data needs to be integrated with other technology (such as Machine Learning) to perform any analysis across the data.

Like all major changes, firms will need a clear business reason for implementing Big Data and it is typically easier to roll out Big Data on a risk-averse phased basis.

Because Big Data is complex then firms need to build an in-house capability to support it. This will cover required technology, suitably skilled staff, and the required governance controls to oversee it.

Big Data is very reliant on data in terms of (a) ensuring the data is timely, complete, and accurate as possible and (b) ensuring compliance with the relevant data protection laws.

Finally, some ethical issues need addressing. While Big Data is normally implemented for the best of reasons, customers and staff will feel uncomfortable if they feel their actions are being monitored. Therefore firms need to be clear and upfront about their usages.

CHAPTER 14

Trend 10—Green Computing

Introduction

Green Computing is part of society's general trend to move to a greener world which is being triggered to combat the very real risk and worry of climate change.

Climate change is caused by society's increased use of burning fossil fuels (such as oil, gas, and coal) which releases greenhouse gases into the atmosphere and acts as a blanket around the globe, stopping the sun's heat from leaving, and therefore increasing global temperatures. These temperature increases will upset the delicate interconnected environmental global eco-system which will then cause changes to long-term shifts in global temperatures and weather patterns which will then, in turn, cause major issues globally with rising sea levels, colder winters, and warmer summers.

There is clear evidence that the world's temperature has increased 1.1°C since the 1800s and it is accepted by nearly all parties that if this trajectory is not reversed then it will cause material issues for current and especially future generations.

Therefore, it could be argued that Green Computing is the most important Technology Trend within this book.

To try and combat this issue then many firms across the economy (i.e., not just financial services firms) are looking to implement "greener" strategies and policies to address these issues. From a Green Computing point-of-view, it covers activities such as using energy-efficient devices, recycling materials, using clean energy, building green buildings plus many others. Green Computing can simply be defined as reducing the adverse environmental impact of technology. This can cover ensuring the physical technology, the processes that support technology, and the people who use the technology are all as green as possible.

It is also worth mentioning ESG (or Environmental, Social, Governance) because more and more firms and investors are using it to determine whether or not to invest in firms. At a simple level, ESG means using a set of factors to measure an organization's holistic capability against a range of variables to observe how well ethically they are running their business (as opposed to just focusing on financial measurements). Please see below:

- Environmental factors cover firms implementing strategies and policies to try and control climate change or "go greener." This is discussed in more detail in the rest of this chapter albeit from a technology point of view.
- Social factors relate to factors to ensuring organizations are socially responsible both internally within their organization and externally with their suppliers, customers, and other stakeholders. It covers areas such as ensuring there is diversity across workforces, any impact to communities is managed, anti-slavery policies are implemented, human rights are managed, consumer protection is in place, and animal rights are considered.
- Governance factors relate to an organization's management. It covers factors such as having an appropriate management structure, risk/control policies and processes implemented, and are fit-for-purpose as well as all staff being remunerated appropriately and fairly.

In effect, ESG could be viewed as some sort of "ethical credit score."

While this sounds good in theory, there are several pragmatic issues regarding this because firms are struggling to obtain consistent, accurate and timely data on firms to allow them to calculate their ESG scores. Therefore, to try and combat this, the European Union (EU) is implementing a new piece of regulation called Sustainable Finance Disclosure Regulation (SFDR) which will try and standardise metrics and reporting. SFDR is discussed in more detail below.

How Financial Services Firms Can Force All Organizations and Governments to Adopt Green Policies

This is not pure technology but it is very relevant to combatting climate change. Financial Services firms have major influence over a wide range of organizations and foreign/local governments which means they should be able to use their collective gravitas to force change for the better.

Ensuring that Organizations Implement Greener Policies

Firms have real influence over many organizations globally through the following activities:

1. Firms (or asset managers specifically) managing holdings on behalf of investors: These investors can range from small individuals to large institutional investors such as mutual funds, insurance funds, or pension funds. As part of this management, Asset Managers will have the ability to vote on these holdings which will give them significant power over the holdings' business direction (especially around improving their approach to climate change). While it is challenging to obtain accurate statistics, it is safe to say around 70 percent of the global stock markets are held by Institutional investors.

2. Firms' normal day-to-day business activity (such as lending money, providing insurance, raising capital, and so on): Bloomberg produced a 2021 report which claimed that emissions associated with financial institutions' normal business activity (of investing, lending, and underwriting activities for their clients) are more than 700 times higher than their direct emissions of running their businesses (such as heat from data centers, heat from buildings, flying staff around the world and so on). The reported figure was ~1.04 gigatons of CO_2 or circa 3 percent of global emissions in 2020. Although the true figure is almost definitely higher because (a) not all financial services firms were included in the data and (b) many firms have probably under-estimated the climate impact of the day-to-day business.

Therefore, financial service firms should be able to actively work together to use this influence to jointly pressure their clients and other organizations to develop and implement green strategies. These strategies do not just cover green computing but they need to cover all aspects of an organizations' business. For example, buildings, factories, transport, supply chains, distribution channels, their suppliers, and so on.

However, as mentioned in the Introduction above, firms and investors are struggling to obtain consistent, accurate, and timely data to measure how "green" (or not) an organization is. Therefore to try and address this the EU is implemented new regulation called Sustainable Finance Disclosure Regulation (SFDR) to force firms, who operate in the EU, to publish both (a) a range of sustainability risks and metrics associated with their products and investments and (b) details of any policies and procedures at the entity level in place to manage the risks. It is hoped that this regulation will ensure that EU investors have the required sustainability metrics and details required to make any investment decisions.

1. Entity level (such as the investment manager or bank): Disclosures will need to be made for the entity covering their policies on decision making around sustainability risks.
2. Product level (such as the individual mutual funds or other investment products): There will be reporting demands are regarding the firms' financial products and their sustainability risks. This means that firms will need to obtain accurate data on the (sometimes hundreds or thousands) investments in their products. Once this data has been collected and consumed then the firm will need to process it and classify their product into one of the three "buckets."

1. Dark Green (or Article 9) products: These are products with a sustainable investment strategy.
2. Light Green (or Article 8) products: These are products that promote environmental or social characteristics to an extent but are not sustainable.

3. Gray (or Article 6) products: These are products that do not integrate any kind of sustainability into their investment process. These can still be sold within the EU but they need to be clearly labeled as non-sustainable. It is expected that these products will be challenged to sell because investors will be looking for more "greener" or sustainable funds.

Classifying products accurately into one of these three buckets will not be easy. This is because timely, complete, and accurate data across the many holdings and investments within these products will be required. This means data will be required from multiple vendors and sources (who will all use different assumptions, coding, and rules). Therefore, a process of data cleansing, normalization, and consolidation will be required to calculate an overall rating.

SFDR will also require a large amount of non-financial and subjective data that will be hard to standardize accurately. Furthermore, this non-financial subjective data may not be widely available for the smaller investments held so any data that is made available could be out-of-date which will impact its accuracy and completeness.

Finally, SFDR requires a firm to provide details on their data collection process which means any issues (like the above) will need to be made public which cause embarrassment or result in external parties (such as customers and the trade press) asking awkward questions.

SFDR came into force on March 10, 2021; all EU firms are now obliged by law to comply with the reporting above. At the time of writing, non-EU companies are not covered by SFDR, it is expected that other jurisdictions (such as the United States and the UK) will implement similar rules and regulations.

As a side note, SFDR has triggered some interesting discussions regarding what firms should do regarding investments that have low SFDR scores. One side of the argument is that firms should sell these holdings because investors will not buy the firms' products. But by disinvesting, does not mean that these firms will change their behaviors and they will continue to adversely impact climate change. The other side of the argument is that firms should keep these holdings and proactive work with offending investment to force them to take active steps to change their behaviors to ensure they become "greener" or more sustainable.

Ensuring that Local/Foreign Governments and Policymakers Implement Greener Policies

In a similar vein, financial service firms should also be able to actively work together to use their joint influence to pressure both local and foreign governments and policymakers to define and implement green policies and tough legislation which will have severe penalties if organizations fail to comply.

Challenges for Financial Services Firms Adopting Green Computing

There are a variety of challenges regarding implementing green computing.

Firms Need to Measure and Benchmark Their Current Green Computing Impact Immediately

Unfortunately, the phrase "going green" or Green Computing is very vague and as a result subjective. Therefore, some quantitative method needs to be used to measure the environmental impact of a firm's technology infrastructure. This infrastructure should not just cover the firm's internal arrangements but also their suppliers and customers (although some firms may feel nervous about approaching customers regarding this).

Measuring the impact can be challenging because there are so many different variables but typically the following areas need to be assessed:

- Power consumption across hardware: for example, PCs, laptops, data centers, and other devices.
- The energy efficiency of buildings and property: for example building power, lighting, lifts, and so on.
- The number of materials that can be recycled: for example paper, hardware, water, buildings, and so on.

Firms could perform this assessment themselves but they could be accused of underestimating any poor ratings. Therefore, it is best to use external auditors to perform this assessment. In an ideal world, it would be advantageous to use more than one external with more than one measurement methodology to ensure there is a wider calculation of the impact.

Once the assessment (or assessments) are complete then the figures can be used as a benchmark or baseline.

Firms Need to Use the Benchmark to Implement a Green Computing Strategy to Reduce Their Impact to a More Acceptable Level

Once the benchmark is calculated (see "Firms Need to Measure and Benchmark Their Current Green Computing Impact Immediately" on page 190) then firms need to design a Green Computing Strategy that will reduce the current assessment to something more acceptable. This strategy will need to include the following:

- A list of actions that need to be implemented: for example use virtual technology or recycle. (See "Implementing Green Computing Involves a Large Number of Small Changes" on page 192 below.)
- A timeline to complete the work thus assuring the impact is reduced.
- A set of interim milestones and measures to ensure progress can be tracked regularly (such as reducing the impact of 10 percent by Year 1, 25 percent by Year 2, etc.)
- A set of policies that define the Green Computing policies and procedures for both internally, the firm's suppliers, and customers.

(This Green Computing Strategy should be part of wider firmwide "green-ness strategy" that will cover all aspects of the firm's operation such as its technology, its operating model, its range of products as well as its suppliers and customers (although, as noted above, trying to change customers can sometimes be challenging).)

Implementing Green Computing Involves a Large Number of Small Changes

There are a variety of activities that a firm could perform to reduce the environmental impact (across their other operations as well as suppliers and customers).

Laptops, Printers, PCs, and so on

All new desktop hardware purchased should be energy efficient and (if possible) they should be configured to hibernate or even power down when not in use. Also, for computer monitors, they should configured to reduce brightness when not in use.

Use Virtual Technology

This involves running several "virtual" servers on a single piece of hardware server as opposed to running a service on its hardware service. This ensures that less hardware is used (with a resultant drop in power usage). However, there is a cost and effort required to move applications onto a virtual infrastructure in terms of new skills required, application changes, testing, and new policies/procedures to support it.

If Virtual Technology Is Not Possible Then Look to Use Spare Capacity on Existing Services

For some (normally older) applications it is not possible to run them on virtual servers which mean firms should look to run multiple applications on servers to ensure full processing capacity is used. This means that less hardware is used (with a resultant drop in power usage) and/or unneeded capacity can be removed.

Look to Minimize Data Storage

Firms should look to reduce data storage usage because it will reduce power usage. This means firms need to look at compression, using

WORM (Write Once Read Many) devices, and looking to achieve data if not needed. However, this may require changes to applications (with associated costs and effort).

Reducing Printing Volumes

Firms should look to print less and use features such as print preview and printing on both sides of the paper. Also, firms should look to use recycled paper. This means less power is used by printers and paper is re-used.

Data Centers

As mentioned above, servers are a large user of power which is exaggerated if servers' full capacity is not used. However, firms should also look at their data centers by looking to implement cooling systems, reusing the heat from the data center (e.g., to heat buildings), and moving to Cloud computing because they are typically more energy efficient.

Applications Should Be Enhanced to Make Them More Efficient

Process-heavy applications (such as the end of data jobs or in-depth analysis) should be reviewed to see if they can be made more efficient. This will reduce process demands which will, in turn, reduce power needs.

Aggressively Implement Recycling Across the Business

Firms should look to implement aggressive recycling policies across the business. This should cover hardware, paper, and so on.

Staff Should Be Educated

Staff should be educated about the importance of Green Computing, the firm's strategy as well as the targets and activities that need to be performed. This is to ensure they have awareness of what needs to be done.

Purchase Only From "Green Computing" Companies

Firms should look to only work with suppliers who have Green Computing in place (or have a clear and demonstrable plan to implement it). For existing suppliers then this may require the firm to put pressure on them to change behaviors with the threat of moving if action is performed.

Only Onboard "Green" Customers

This is a notoriously tricky area because Firms generally do not like to pressure or upset clients. But some firms are looking to assess the "greenness" of their clients (especially the large institutional-type clients) and if they are not as green as they should be then they will either not on-board them or, if they are an existing client, look to change the customer's behavior or even offload them.

Green Computing Will Not Be Cheap and Will Take Time

Implementing Green Computing (or trying to go green generally) is not an easy activity. It will involve firms making changes internally (such as virtualization, buying new PCs, and enhancing applications) as well as working and putting pressure on suppliers and possibly clients. This means that it costs money and will require people and effort across the organization to implement. This means that senior management needs to be aware that this could divert money and resources from other activities.

It Is Possible to Use Going Green as a Selling Point or Competitive Advantage

Some firms are using "going green" as a competitive advantage. They will boast about their energy-efficient buildings and technology or they have launched green products which only invest in green companies where the administration is green (such as all statements printed on recycled paper). This is a good message to send to the market place and it is also helpful in keeping existing and attracting new customers.

However, there is a risk that if the firm presents itself as "green" and issues are found then this will create bad PR which could take a while to recover from and create a general lack of trust in the firm as well as the wider Financial Services industry.

Emerging Technologies Require a Large Amount of Processing Power

The majority of the emerging technologies discussed in this textbook require both large amounts of processing (such as Machine Learning, Big Data, and Digital Currency) and specific hardware (such as Remote Working, Self-Servicing, and the Internet of Things). Therefore, firms need to be aware of this because by implementing new technology they could be inadvertently increasing the environmental impact.

Future Challenges

Table 14.1 Future challenges of Green Computing

Area	Details
Increased regulations	This area will be adversely impacted as firms will need to cope with increasingly more "green-related regulation." As the importance of "going green" increases then regulators are implementing regulations (such as the EU's SFDR) which firms will need to comply with, with severe penalties for non-compliance.
Changing nature of clients	Firms will need to monitor clients' reactions to going green. Global warming is now a massive issue with a large amount of genuine and warranted worry. Customers (especially the younger demographics) may not want to deal with firms (or any suppliers) who are not genuinely implementing changes to reduce their environmental impact. Therefore, if firms do not implement Green Computing as well as wider green changes then, apart from contributing to global warming, firms will lose customers.

(Continued)

Table 14.1 (Continued)

Evolution of products	Firms will need to ensure that all their products are green because otherwise, investors will long term ignore them. This means having products that only invest in green companies where the administration is green (such as all statements printed on recycled paper).
Lack of trust	If the financial services industry thinks carefully about "going green" then it could increase trust in the industry. Financial Services firms (as investors, voting power, and service providers) have a large amount of influence across the global economy. Therefore, they should be able to use this power to "force" organizations to implement changes to ensure they are green. There is a real opportunity for financial services to be a leading light in these areas.
Accurate data	This area will be adversely impacted in two main areas. Firstly, to ensure that firms fully understand their environmental impact then they will need to measure their performance. This will require using new data feeds which will be costly and complex to consume and process. Secondly, allow firms to accurately classify their products (such as into the Dark Green, Light Green, and Gray buckets under SFDR) then firms will need timely, accurate, and complete data on holdings within their products. This data will be challenging to obtain (especially for some often smaller holdings) and even more challenging to process to ensure there are consistent assessments.
Poor operating and technology models	There will be an adverse impact on operating models. Existing complex and stretched operating models will need to be (a) enhanced to ensure they are green and also (b) monitored regularly. This means operating models become more complex, costly, and risky to maintain.
Profitability/Cost drivers	Profitability will be impacted (at least in the short term). Implementing Green Technology will cost money in the short to medium term which will impact profitability. Senior management at firms will need to be aware of this and accept it. Also if a firm is not as green as its competitors then it could lose business to them. Thus, impacting revenue lines and overall profitability.
Changing nature of the workforce	There will be opportunities for staff in these areas. New skills will be required to support Green Computing such as virtualization and cloud computing.

New competition and replacements	This area is a threat to existing firms. As mentioned earlier, "going green" can be viewed as a selling point and can be used to keep existing customers and attract new customers. Larger firms with ageing operating models will take longer to implement Green Computing than smaller or more nimble competitors. This means they could lose market share.
Risk profile	This area will be adversely impacted. There is real pressure for firms to implement green strategies (not just Green Computing) to reduce their environmental impact. If this is not actioned then firms will lose business and be at risk for any future green regulations.

Case Study

The majority of the activity that firms are performing to implement Green Computing is very similar (such as implementing virtualization or looking to aggressively recycle); however, there are a couple of innovative implementations some firms are investigating, viz:

- One firm is looking to use the heat generated from their in-house data center to warm the water supply within their offices.
- Another firm is looking to implement an onsite paper recycling capability where they recycle all their paper on-premise.

Summary

It can easily be argued that Green Computing is possibly the most important emerging technology in this book. If global warming is not reversed or halted then it will cause irreparable damage to the entire planet.

While firms are generally looking to implement Green Computing across themselves, their suppliers, and possibly customers, the biggest advantage that Financial Services have is that they have a large amount of influence across the global economy (as investors, voting power, and service providers). Therefore, financial service firms should be able to actively work together (a) to pressure these organizations and their boards to develop and implement green strategies and (b) to pressure both local and foreign governments and policymakers to define and implement green policies and tough legislation which will have severe penalties if organizations fail to comply.

CHAPTER 15

Wrap Up and Looking to the Future

Introduction

This final chapter is split into two main parts.

The first section provides a high-level summary of the challenges that Financial Services firms will need to address to increase the likelihood of successfully implementing the new emerging technologies listed.

The second section provides a summary of how the emerging technologies can either help or hinder the challenges of the financial services that were documented in Chapter 4 at the start of this book.

Summary of Key Themes and Challenges

This first section provides a high-level summary of the challenges that Financial Services firms will need to address to increase the likelihood of successfully implementing the new emerging technologies listed.

Firms Need a Clear Business Reason to Implement Any Technology

There are many stories of firms (not just in the Financial Services) implementing new technology for the sake of the technology as opposed to implementing technology to meet some type of business or strategic need.

This means before embarking on a technology implementation (whether is an emerging technology or not) then a firm must have a clear business reason to implement the technology. These implementations need to be viewed as a large strategic change and will need to be treated with the same amount of respect.

New Technology Should Be Implemented Gradually

There is a clear tendency to try and implement new technology too quickly. This is because people get "carried away with the technology." This is especially true in Financial Services. However, implementing any new technology is a challenging process and it should be taken gradually with regular point reviews.

Therefore, it is normally advisable to perform some sort of pilot implementation to assess does the technology work?, does it offer the benefits promised?, and does the firm have the skills to implement the technology? The results of the pilot study can inform the rest of the implementation although even once the pilot study is completed then a gradual rollout plan should be implemented. This allows the firm to understand the technology and associated impacts as well as build confidence, momentum, and a return on investment with senior management.

Do Not Under-Estimate the Regulatory Complexity When Implementing Technology

Financial Services is currently governed by a complex set of regulations. It is also expected that the amount and complexity of regulation will continue to increase for the foreseeable future.

While there is little specific regulation regarding the technology trends covered in this book (although this could change if any of the technologies become mainstream or there are significant issues with technologies), there is still a sizeable amount of existing regulation that is very relevant. For example, complex data protection legislation across many jurisdictions, increasing operational resilience regulation, increased sustainability regulation in the EU and recently published guidelines around Cloud Computing.

Therefore, when implementing new technology (or making any change to it) then it is important that firms fully understand the regulatory landscape and ensure that they are accommodated for it during implementation.

(At a general level, firms need to have a regulatory compliance intelligence or research capability where they constantly monitor for new, changed, or removed regulation so they can make the necessary changes to the product base and operating models to ensure they continue to comply).

Firms Need to Be Aware of the Growing Cyber Risk Challenge

A number of the technology trends require firms to open their technology infrastructure to the outside world. For example, remote working allows staff access to nearly all parts of a firm's technology to perform their work. Likewise, if a firm uses Internet of Things (IoT) devices to provide self-servicing then this will mean many different devices which will be running different operating systems and applications will have access to the inner parts of the firm's infrastructure.

This means firms are at risk of a variety of problems such as viruses, Trojan horses, phasing, denial-of-service, password attacks, SQL injection attacks plus many others. If these issues are not managed properly then the firm is at risk of a variety of major problems. For example, customers' accounts being hacked and their money being removed, client personal data being stolen, technology systems being unavailable, and a significant loss of reputation in the marketplace.

Therefore, when implementing new technology it is important that security measures (covering technology changes, people being suitably skilled, and the required processes and policies) are designed as part of the implementation and not added as an after-thought at the end.

There Are Also Other Risks Than Just Cyber Risk

In addition to Cyber Risk (see above), the new technology will negatively impact all risks that could impact a firm. For example, adding new technology increases operational risk because the technology and operating model is more complex. Secondly, the new technology is very reliant on data so a firm's data risk increases. Furthermore, this complexity will increase the regulatory burden on a firm and its associated risks. Finally, a firm's financial risk profile will increase because (while most of the technologies will reduce costs or increase revenue) there is often a long payback period which could be impacted if circumstances change in the environment (such as regulatory change or major drop in market values).

Therefore, similar to Cyber Security, when implementing new technology all risks must be assessed and managed during the implementation to ensure they are mitigated as much as possible before implementation. Risk management should not be covered as an after-thought.

New Skills and Capabilities Will Be Required

The new technologies will require firms to develop new skills and capabilities to support them. This does not just cover the technology staff "on the ground" who will develop, implement, and support the technology, but also senior management who will need to understand the technology because it will allow them to how it could be used strategically going forward.

If a firm does not develop these skills then it will always be reliant on external contractors, consultants, and software vendors.

Therefore, when a new technology is being implemented then the project plan must ensure that the required skills are developed in-house before go-live.

Staff Losing Their Jobs Is Part of a New Technology Implementation

On the opposing side to the section above, it may be necessary for staff to lose their jobs when new technology is being implemented. This is not pleasant for all parties involved. Therefore, it is important as part of the implementation that if staff are losing their jobs then tasks must be scheduled to ensure that process is as "pain-free" as possible and that staff departing are treated as tactfully as possible and that all relevant legislation is followed correctly.

Firms Need to Build a Robust Infrastructure to Support the New Technologies

To ensure that the technology can work then firms need to develop a robust infrastructure to support new technology.

This can be looked at as four parts:

- The new technology itself will need to be implemented and each of them has its challenges in regards to hosting and support. However one of the biggest challenges is that the new technology will need to integrate with existing technology infrastructure (which itself is a complex "patchwork quilt" of new systems, old systems, in-house systems, supplier systems, manual integrations, etc.). In effect, more complexity is being overlaid on already existing complexity.

- New operational business processes will need to be designed and implemented to run the new technology. For example, processes for managing NLP rejections or procedures for investigating Know-Your-Client failures. Again this will no doubt involve updating already complex business processes.

- New oversight and governance controls will need to be implemented to oversee the system. This will need to cover managing the risks mentioned (such as Cyber), ensuring the suppliers are monitored for performing, ensuring that BCP tests are performed satisfactorily, and so on are completed when required plus many other items.

- Finally (and has been discussed earlier) firms will need to ensure they have suitably skilled people to develop and support the new technologies.

For nearly all firms, updating their operating model is a massive and challenging activity. This means that when looking to implement new technology firms fully investigate what needs to be done before committing to implementation costs and deadlines. Also during implementation firms will need to monitor the progress of this work to ensure that any issues and slippage are identified immediately so they can be addressed quickly.

Data Is Now Even More Key Than It Was Originally

Data is already a massive part of Financial Services and all firms currently struggle with ensuring that they can obtain complete, timely, and accurate data as well as ensuring that they can process it as required.

However, all the new technologies detailed in this book will increase the strain and importance of data. This will require more data and more complex processing.

There is a variety of examples. NLP will need constantly updated lexicons to ensure it can continue to "understand" what it is being told. Self-servicing needs accurate client data otherwise it will not be able to service clients. Machine learning needs (a very large amount of) data for the development and testing of its algorithms and models. Firms will need accurate data on both their operations and their products' investments to allow the "green" or sustainable scores to be calculated.

Therefore as part of technology implementation, firms will need to clearly understand what data is required and where they can obtain it. This will then allow them to develop technology, processes, controls, and so on to ensure the data is sourced by go live.

New Technologies Have Social Acceptance Issues

At a general level, there is always some type of social acceptance for new technology or change generally. For example, it took many years for Automated Teller Machines (ATM) to be accepted by all parts of society.

This is no different for new emerging technology.

This means that firms need to be aware that some of the customers, staff and other market participants may be uncomfortable with the new technology. For example, some customers (mainly older generally) are ill at ease speaking to a computer so if a firm is implementing NLP for client servicing then it will need to ensure there is an option for the customer to speak to a "human." Likewise, some customers are unhappy with using digital currencies so a firm may still need to support cheques, notes, and coins. Finally, a large number of people are nervous about firms using Machine Learning techniques to try and manipulate them which means firms will need to be very clear on how Machine Learning is being used for.

Therefore, as part of the implementation, firms will need to think about whether implementing new technology will cause any social acceptance issues and make necessary provisions for them before go-live.

The New Technologies Interact and Rely on Each Other

While this book tends to discuss and debate the technologies in isolation, it is important to stress that all the emerging technologies do interact with and rely on each other.

For example, Machine Learning will need input data to allow it to run its models and this input data could be provided from a Natural Language Processing website, self-servicing, or a variety of IoT devices. Once this data has been received then it will need to be stored somewhere which will need Big Data (which in turn needs Cloud computing to host it because of the vast amount). Finally, once the models have been run then the results need to be outputted somewhere and this could be an NLT response, self-servicing response, or an update on an IoT device.

Therefore, firms need to be aware that if they are looking to implement a new emerging technology then they may need to implement other technologies to allow it to work.

Looking Forward to How the Emerging Trends Can Help or Hinder the Financial Services Industry

This final section provides a summary of how the emerging technologies holistically can either help or hinder the challenges of the financial services that were documented in Chapter 4 at the start of this book.

Therefore, in summary, it can be said that the new technologies provide real benefits for customers (through improved servicing and products as well as increased choice from new entrants) but they will cause material problems for firms regarding the operating models, ability to support the required data and their risk profile. There are also issues around regulation, trust, cost/profitability, and workforce changes that are hard to predict accurately at the moment.

Table 15.1 Summary of future challenges for the financial services industry

Area	Impact	Details
Increased regulations		This area is neutral at the moment from a technology point. Regarding specific technology regulations. There is some general regulation at the moment (about Data Protection, Operational Resilience, and Cloud Computing) which firms need to comply with. However, if any of the technologies either become more mainstream or there are public or material issues with them then it is very likely that regulation will follow. However, this is still a constant flow of new and complex general financial services regulations. This flow will continue to last for many years and it will impact all parts of firms (and not just technology).
Changing nature of clients		This area is benefitted by the new technologies. The emerging technologies allow better customer servicing, improved products, and (albeit longer-term) reducing fees.
Evolution of products		Similar to "Changing Nature of Clients" this area is benefitted from the new technologies. The emerging technologies allow better customer servicing, improved products, and (albeit longer-term) reducing fees.
Lack of trust		This area is neutral at the moment (although one could argue that trust in Financial Services is so low at the moment that it could not get any worse). The new emerging technologies will improve the customer experience which should improve trust in firms and the wider Financial Services industry. However, customers and the general public may be skeptical about the new technologies. For example, are firms using Machine Learning to manipulate clients? Or some people are unhappy speaking to an NLP-supported computer. Therefore, firms will need to carefully manage the message about why the technology is implemented and how it will benefit customers because otherwise customers and the general public could think that firms are implementing the changes for their selfish benefits.

Accurate data		This area is impacted negatively in a major way. All firms rely on data and most firms currently struggle with ensuring the required data is complete, timely, and accurate. The new technologies increase pressure on firms for more data (such as ensuring NLP lexicons are up-to-date or there is sufficient data for SFDR assessments). This means that firms will need to develop capabilities to source the data as well as to correctly process it.
Poor operating and technology models		This area is impacted negatively in a major way. All firms already have a complex operating model which consists of a "patchwork quilt" of new systems, old systems, in-house systems, supplier systems, manual processes, spreadsheets, etc. Implementing new technology will only add more complexity, risk, and strain to these models. Therefore, firms will need to ensure the technology, process, people, and oversight are suitably robust to cope with the extra pressures.
Profitability/Cost drivers		The impact for this item is neutral. At a general level, long-term, all the new technologies bar two (namely Remote Working and Green Computing) will either reduce operating costs and/or increase revenue. Although all implementations will have a long payback period which could make some firms nervous because the longer the payback period then the greater the risk of the environment changing and negatively impacting the business case. Regarding the two technologies that are just a cost. • Remote working will cost firms money to implement and it is unlikely to generate revenue but it could improve the welfare of staff by improving their work-life balance and well-being. • Green Computing will cost a firm to implement and may generate some revenue in the short-term if the firms offer "green" products, but will not generate any significant revenue in the long term once the entire industry has gone green.

(Continued)

Table 15.1 (Continued)

Changing nature of the workforce		The impact for this item is neutral. New skills will be needed to support the new technologies which will provide a development opportunity. However, some existing staff will lose their jobs due to their activity being replaced by computers. Also, remote working will allow staff to have a much better work-vs.-life balance because it will allow staff the opportunity to work from home.
New competition and replacements		This area is impacted beneficially for customers and new entrants (but is a concern for existing firms). The new technologies will allow new entrants to enter the financial services quicker, cheaper, and with innovative functionally rich products. This will benefit them as well as customers because it gives them a better range of products. However, this is a threat to existing firms because they will need to react and change the products and business models to cope with these new entrants.
Risk profile		This area is impacted negatively. While new technology allows better control over processes and customers, they do significantly increase the risk profile of firms. There are increased risks around data, operating models, possible new regulations, costs management, cyber, and many other areas. This means firms will need to develop capabilities to identify and manage risks over a wide range of areas.

Appendix A

Supplier Selection Checklist

For most technologies, a supplier or vendor will likely be used to provide some part of the system. For example infrastructure, application code, support, and so on. This means it is important that care and attention are taken when selecting a supplier.

The entire process can be defined as follows:

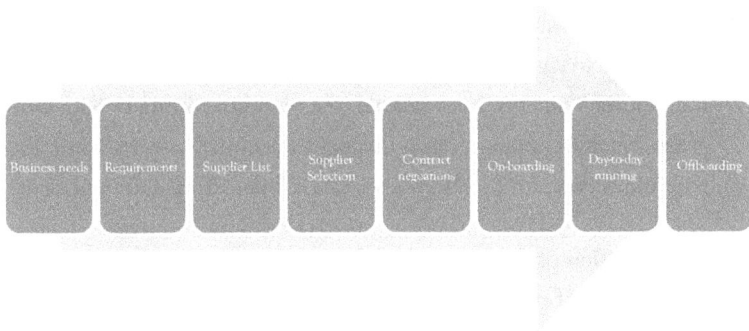

Figure A.1 Supplier selection, implementation, and off-boarding lifecycle

Confirm the Business Need

The first stage is to confirm the business need for the supplier selection. For example, a Cloud computing provider is required because the firm wants to reduce day to day technology costs by XYZ percent or a Machine Learning platform is required to reduce the number of trading errors.

Also at this stage, it is advisable to confirm which staff are needed (a) to be involved in the supplier selection process and (b) to be involved as some sort of senior management forum to oversee and eventually approve the supplier selection.

Confirm the Requirements That Need to Be Assessed as Part of the Selection

This stage involves creating a list of requirements that need to be assessed during the supplier selection. This can cover a wide range of areas but the following groups tend to cover what is needed:

1. Functional fit.

   It needs to be clear what functionality the platform is offering and does this functionality meet the firm's needs. However, it is important to remember that some platforms may have too much functionality for some of the smaller or less complex firms. Therefore do not be afraid of choosing a platform that does not have the range of features as other larger platforms (as long as it meets the firm's needs).

2. Integration with the firm's current systems.

   Firms need to ensure that the selected platform can easily integrate with their current systems. For example, the platform integrates with older green screen technology, can it link with the e-mail systems, can it link with old versions of MS-Windows, can it link to FTP sites, and so on.

3. Confirmation of the support model.

   In the event of problems then what help desk or support model is in place? What are its service levels? What hours does it operate? And so on. Does this level of service meet the firm's needs and requirements?

4. Hosting of the platform.

   The technology platform will need to be hosted on some type of servers. Asking the supplier to host the platform often sounds easier but this does cause an issue, namely:

   • What is their support model?
   • In what location will the data be stored?
   • What are the supplier's information security policies?
   • Is the data encrypted?
   • Does the supplier charge an extra fee for this?
   • What are BCP arrangements?

However, if the platform has to be hosted internally then

- What hardware and skills are needed?
- How easy it is to obtain these skills?
- How expensive will this be?

5. Ensure that all costs are clearly understood.

Most suppliers will charge some sort of upfront fee plus an annual license fee. Therefore, it is important to understand how much these fees are and what is covered (or not covered by them).

If there are any "extras" then what are they and how much do they cost? However, the supplier must be making a reasonable profit from the contract. A firm cannot afford for a supplier to go out of business because it will impact the firm's operating model, product offering, and so on.

6. Ensure everything is covered in the contract.

Everything agreed upon in the vendor selection process must be included in the contract. In other words, firms need to be sure that all the functionality demonstrated and promises made during the sales process have been included in the contract and no key features are "extras" that will need to be paid for at a later date.

While this may seem cumbersome it is important because if there are legal disputes then the content of the contract becomes key.

The following specific legal points should also be covered:

- Direct or indirect (or consequential) loss—in effect if there are monetary, regulatory, legal, or reputational errors caused then who pays for them. For example the firm, the provider, or a combination of both.
- Termination clauses—a suitable timeline needs to be included which ensures (a) the firm can leave relatively quickly if they want to migrate a way and (b) the vendor cannot terminate without giving the firm sufficient time to find and move to a new platform.

- Confidentiality agreement—this is normally two-way and ensures both sides do not share confidential information with other parties.
- Protection of Intellectual Property—this clause will ensure that if any ideas, bots, and so on are developed then they are not sold or reused by other firms who use the platform.

7. Ensure any critical dates or full timeline is agreed upon.
   If the platform provider is helping with the implementation (such as providing consultancy, developing / test software, implementing hosting, and project management) then all key dates with clear roles and responsibilities for delivery should be included in the contract.

8. Cultural fit with the supplier.
   Finally, there needs to be a good cultural fit between the firm and the selected platform provider. Because the roll-out of the technology is important then the selected provider will be a key strategic supplier and will work with the firm closely for many years. This means there needs to be good culture and working fit between the two. Otherwise, there will be problems and tension.
   Trying to assess a cultural fit can be challenging but the following may help:

   - Who are the supplier's other customers (especially the financial services ones)? Are they similar to your firm? Can you arrange to speak to them to understand how the supplier operates and so on? If they note any issues then these need to be investigated before anything is signed.
   - Try and arrange to meet supplier staff who the firm will work with on a day-to-day basis? After meeting these people then do you feel a good cultural fit? If not then is the supplier willing the change the staff members?

9. Prepare for Exit Planning
   The supplier arrangement could terminate in one of three ways namely (a) the firm terminates the agreement (b) the supplier terminates the agreement or (c) the supplier stops offering the service

abruptly, say due to bankruptcy, and firms need to have plans to find an instant replacement.

For the first two items (namely (a) and (b)) the contract needs to include a comprehensive Exit Plan that provides sufficient time for both parties to exit the arrangement and, if necessary, find alternative arrangements. This Exit Plan will need to contain details on roles, responsibilities, return of data, and timelines, and ensure that there are no interruptions in service.

For the final item (namely (c)) the firm needs to have pre-made plans that can be immediately executed if the supplier fails. This could be having an alternative supplier in place which could be used immediately, having a supplier ready to go but will need time to be ready or even looking at closing down a part of the business.

10. Does the firm have audit rights?

The contract should have wording to allow the firm to audit the supplier regularly. The frequency of the audit will depend on the importance or risk of the arrangement. High risk or more important suppliers will be audited more regularly than others.

The audit will allow firms to ensure that the supplier is still able to meet their obligations in the contract. For example, the audit could cover reviewing performance, technology, processes, people, management, governance, risk management, finances, cyber-securities, the supplier's suppliers plus any other relevant areas.

11. How reliant is the supplier on using other suppliers (or 4th parties)

Nearly all suppliers are reliant on other providers and vendors to provide the service being offered. This could cover anything from using external software packages, using outsourced administrators, employing agency staff, and so on.

However, it is important when selecting a supplier that a firm fully understands what parts of the service being provided are dependent on the supplier's suppliers. If these elements are critical then the firm should ensure they investigate and oversee these parts regularly. Also, the firm may insist the supplier agrees to any changes to these 4th parties before any changes are made.

12. What regulatory notification and approvals are needed?

    Depending on the suppliers being procured then it may be necessary to inform the relevant regulators about a change of supplier. This notification could range from asking permission or confirming a change has been made once it has gone live. Therefore firms and suppliers need to ensure that they factor in regulatory approvals or notifications.

Create a List of Suppliers to Be Assessed

A list of suppliers to be assessed needs to be created. This list can be created from speaking to existing staff, speaking with trade bodies or specialist consultancies who know this area. However, there is a possibility that only one supplier is available.

Perform an Assessment of the Suppliers' Capabilities Against the List of Requirements

This step involves the firm speaking to the suppliers (or single supplier) listed (see "Create a list of suppliers to be assessed" directly above) and assessing them against the list of requirements created (in "Confirm the requirements that need to be assessed as part of the selection" on page 210). The assessment is typically done by the firm asking each supplier to complete a questionnaire (or request for proposal) in a formal manner which is then followed by several meetings and workshops to address and drill into any specific points.

At the end of this process then a recommended supplier or suppliers can be selected to move into the contract and detailed due diligence phase. While it is not uncommon for more than one supplier to move into the next stage, firms need to be mindful that having more than one firm will create a large amount of work which may not be that beneficial.

Detailed Contract Negotiation, Due Diligence, and Reverse Due Diligence

Once the preferred supplier (or suppliers) is selected then the firm will need to perform detailed contract negations to ensure all the requirements, legal clauses, and so on are included in the contract.

This work may require the firm to perform detailed due diligence on the supplier to ensure everything that has been suggested earlier can be performed. This could cover performance, technology, processes, people, management, governance, risk management, finances, cyber-securities, the supplier's suppliers plus any other relevant areas.

Likewise, for certain contracts, the supplier may want to perform (reverse) due diligence on the firm to ensure everything the firm has stated is fully correct and valid.

Beware of losing all goodwill during the contract negotiations. While it is very prudent for the firm and the supplier to ensure they have negotiated the best deal for themselves, it is also important to ensure they both sides do not negotiate so aggressively that they have lost all "good will" (and effectively "hate"' each other) before the contract is signed. Remember signing the contract is the first stage and both parties will need to work with each other for many years going forward.

Finally (as mentioned above) you must ensure the suppliers is making a reasonable profit from the contract. A firm cannot afford for a supplier to go out of business because it will impact the firm's operating model, product offering and so on. This means the supplier must make some profit from the arrangement.

Onboard the Supplier

This step involves onboarding the new supplier arrangement. This could range from a simple process of "flicking on the switch" (say for using a new trading partner) to a complex lengthy implementations spanning several years (such as a migration of data centers to the Cloud). Also as part of this stage, it may be necessary to off-board existing suppliers.

Day-to-Day Running

Once the supplier is onboarded then the arrangement can go live.

This will involve using the supplier on the required regular basis. For example using their Cloud platform, using their NLP technology or trading with them.

As part of this, there will need to be some sort of regular oversight and tracking of the supplier. The scope, depth, and frequency of this will depend on the criticality of the supplier but typically it will cover reviewing performance, technology, processes, people, management, governance, risk management, finances, cyber-securities, the supplier's suppliers plus any other relevant areas.

Exiting the Supplier Arrangement

As mentioned earlier the supplier arrangement could terminate in one of three ways namely (a) the firm terminates the agreement (b) the supplier terminates the agreement or (c) the supplier stops offering the service immediately, say due to bankruptcy, and the firm needs to find an instant replacement.

For the first two items (namely (a) and (b)) the contract should include a comprehensive Exit Plan that provides sufficient time for both parties to exit the arrangement and, if necessary, find alternative arrangements. Therefore in this situation then is the plan should be followed.

For the final item (name (c)) the firm needs to have pre-made plans that can be immediately executed if the supplier fails. This could be having an alternative supplier in place which could be used immediately, having a supplier ready to go but will need time to be ready or even looking at closing down a part of the business.

Appendix B

Business Case Checklist

It is not uncommon that firms appear to implement new technology for the sake of the technology as opposed to implementing technology to meet some type of business or strategic need.

(In the same way as any major change) this means before starting an implementation then a firm must have a clear business reason to implement it and these reasons must link clearly to the strategy of the firm. For example:

- Cost reduction (such as reducing staff levels or reducing office staff).
- Improving efficiency (such as running certain processes 24 hours per day).
- Reducing errors rates (such as reducing the number of errors by a certain percentage or reducing the cost of errors by a monetary amount).
- Increasing flexibility and making scaling up (or down) to meet volumes quicker and cheaper.
- Plus possible others.

Once a clear business reason has been confirmed then firms need to assess key success criteria. Or in other words, what factors (or key success criteria) have to be met to allow the firm to state that the implementation has been successful (or not). This can cover a wide range of factors (see below) and if there is one than one then the factors will need to be weighted and prioritized:

- Staff reduction by a certain level
- Operating costs reduced by a certain level

- Reducing error levels by a certain amount
- A certain percentage of the process is covered
- Plus others

Once the clear business reason to implement and key success factors are understood then a business case will need to be created, reviewed, and approved by senior management. This business will need to cover the following:

- The costs to implement—this could cover new technology platform required, new data feeds required, new skills that need developing, the cost of the project team, legal costs, and so on.
- The costs to run on a day-to-day basis once live—this could cover technology support costs, the costs of the new team(s) to support, and so on.
- Details of any other costs caused by the implementation. For example, if the implementation is to reduce staffing levels then any redundancy costs should be noted because these could be large.
- Predicted costs savings that will be caused by the implementation. This could cover staff savings, office space savings, reduction in the costs of errors, and so on.
- The payback period—in effect how long will it take for the investment to payback? Or in other words how long will it take for the cost savings and cover the new day-to-day running and all implementation costs. This is sometimes referred to as the Return-on-Investment.
- List of major risks—such as increased reliance on technology, possible problems with implementing new technology, and so on.
- The proposed end state once robotic process automation has been implemented. This could cover staffing levels (especially if reduced), office space, processes that will be moved to bots, technology change, any news processes (such as new oversight processes), and so on.

- Implementation timeline—this plan should dictate the tasks and dependencies that are needed to implement RPA or effectively move the firm from where they are now to the proposed end-state defined above.
- The governance structure for implementation—a senior member of management should be nominated to sponsor and/or champion the implementation. This senior manager should be supported by a wider group of management, covering all impacted areas, who should be able to help with the implementation. An experienced project manager should also be recruited to lead the implementation with support from all impacted areas of the business.

About the Author

Paul Taylor is a consultant with nearly 34 years experience across the financial services, charities, technology, education, and professional bodies industries with specific disciplinary expertise around strategic direction setting, change, technology, operations, product development, outsourcing, governance, and regulation.

Paul is also a Chair/NED for various social and commercial organizations covering performing arts, gambling addiction awareness, education, book reviews, and financial services.

Paul is a published author, speaker and lecturer across many subjects such as change management, freelancing, technology, governance, supplier management, research techniques, culture, financial services, innovation, entrepreneurship, COVID-19 impacts plus others.

Index

OTHER TITLES IN THE SERVICE SYSTEMS AND INNOVATIONS IN BUSINESS AND SOCIETY COLLECTION

Jim Spohrer, IBM, and Haluk Demirkan, University of Washington, Tacoma, Editors

- *The Emergent Approach to Strategy* by Peter Compo
- *Compassion-Driven Innovation* by Nicole Reineke, Debra Slapak, and Hanna Yehuda
- *Adoption and Adaption in Digital Business* by Keith Sherringham and Bhuvan Unhelkar
- *Customer Value Starvation Can Kill* by Walter Vieira
- *Build Better Brains* by Martina Muttke
- *ATOM, Second Edition* by Kartik Gada
- *Designing Service Processes to Unlock Value, Third Edition* by Joy M. Field
- *Disruptive Innovation and Digital Transformation* by Marguerite L. Johnson
- *Service Excellence in Organizations, Volume II* by Fiona Urquhart
- *Service Excellence in Organizations, Volume I* by Fiona Urquhart
- *Obtaining Value from Big Data for Service Systems, Volume II* by Stephen H. Kaisler, Armour, and J. Alberto Espinosa
- *Obtaining Value from Big Data for Service Systems, Volume I* by Stephen H. Kaisler, Armour, and J. Alberto Espinosa

Concise and Applied Business Books

The Collection listed above is one of 30 business subject collections that Business Expert Press has grown to make BEP a premiere publisher of print and digital books. Our concise and applied books are for…

- Professionals and Practitioners
- Faculty who adopt our books for courses
- Librarians who know that BEP's Digital Libraries are a unique way to offer students ebooks to download, not restricted with any digital rights management
- Executive Training Course Leaders
- Business Seminar Organizers

Business Expert Press books are for anyone who needs to dig deeper on business ideas, goals, and solutions to everyday problems. Whether one print book, one ebook, or buying a digital library of 110 ebooks, we remain the affordable and smart way to be business smart. For more information, please visit www.businessexpertpress.com, or contact sales@businessexpertpress.com.

www.ingramcontent.com/pod-product-compliance
Lightning Source LLC
Chambersburg PA
CBHW061158220326
41599CB00025B/4520